D0472497

# LEX FERENDA
(Latin for "what the law should be")

Printed in the United States of America

ISBN 978-0-9839349-0-5

# Lex Ferenda

# CONTENTS

# DEDICATIONS

This book is dedicated in honor of my parents George Dewey and Grace Marie, my wife Dorothy, my sisters for assisting with my upbringing, my brother for giving me a job during college, and to all the teachers responsible for my education.

In addition, I would like to dedicate it to all the conservative think tanks such as The Heritage Foundation, The American Enterprise Institute, etc., and all the conservative radio commentators for their work in trying to inform the public about the foundation of the United States and the republican principles that make it function. Despite their mostly originalist positions, maybe middle-class and stanch conservatives will become convinced of the logic of revising the Constitution in a blue-collar "we the people" manner rather than waiting to see what the elites and liberals might do on their terms at some future date.

Third, a dedication is in order to the youth of the nation in the expectation that the word "posterity" in the Constitution will not be overlooked. Hopefully, the "video generation" will wake up in time to save the basic rules of law and ethics before Congress spends them into the poor house of history.

# PREFACE

This information is included for readers not familiar with the early history of the United States Constitution. A one-page background will help us get started. For a more detailed history see the many other references available in your local library.

In the late 1700s, after many years of abuse by the English Crown of the thirteen American Colonies with respect to taxes and regulations, the colonists began to resist, first with assemblies and the written word, but finally in open rebellion. The hostilities began in Massachusetts in mid 1775, spread throughout the colonies, and ended with the defeat of the British, albeit with French assistance, in October of 1781 at Yorktown, Virginia.

Shortly thereafter the colonies got together and established a Confederation with a Congress in which each colony (State) had one vote. The Confederation of the States[1] lasted only a few years until it became obvious that it was too weak to provide defense, commerce regulation, and other central necessities of a growing country.

In the summer of 1787 some of the leaders of the States got together to consider major amendments to the Articles of Confederation, but it soon became apparent that a better document was necessary to provide all the changes required. In about four months, delegates from the States negotiated and debated in secrecy the contents of a new basic Constitution for the United States and by June of 1788 the document was ratified by nine of the deemed necessary number of States. To solidify citizen and State support, a Bill of Rights (the first ten amendments), was added to the Constitution soon thereafter and ratified sufficiently by the States in December of 1791. Since then, and to the present (mid 2010), seventeen more amendments have been added to the document.

The purpose of this book is to help the reader better understand the Constitution of the United States and hopefully provide reasoning for some changes that may be advantageous. Emphasis is placed on the convention option of Article V.

---

[1] The words State, Constitution, Amendment, and Act are capitalized throughout the book for emphasis.

# INTRODUCTION

After Monica-gate, when the President was not convicted for lying under oath and thereby violating both the law and the Constitution simultaneously, it became obvious that there was something seriously wrong with our legislative body and our political system. Our basic law, the Constitution of the United States, is at the heart of that system. A website was placed on the Internet by the author in 1999 trying to get citizens interested in the problem. Reaction to the website was insufficient; so several years were spent reading and studying literature covering philosophy, government, economics, banking and constitutions, to provide the reference material for Lex Ferenda.

Besides not upholding the law, the problem of congress being inept in money management, regardless of which party is in control, was well documented by 2000. More recently, giant deficits have resulted in a new Tea Party faction and a record low congress rating. This book attempts to convince the reader that the Framers were serious when they placed the "convention option" in Article V of our Constitution and that an unbiased convention can and should be held with the States leading the way.

If you come to agree with me that the Constitution of the United States has some serious flaws you will likely be interested in this book's conclusions. On the other hand, if you feel the Constitution is much like the Bible, set in stone, and should not be questioned, then it may be difficult to lead you through the analysis and conclusions. But I'm determined to try, so please read on and be patient.

Also be aware, the author is not a professional writer, but an engineer and military officer by profession. I've taken the military officer fact as a tacit approval to tackle this project since many of the Founders/Framers were officers in the Revolutionary War. I do wholeheartedly support our present Constitution, having taken an oath to do so, and will continue that pledge until a modernized document is properly ratified. But it also seems reasonable to assume that "upholding" our basic law implies approval of a stronger and better Constitution.

The book has been arranged to address background information first and then consider the main body of the Constitution. To trim length I have left out frequent quotes by common references used in this type of book, such as those of Baron de Montesquieu, John Locke, etc. Readers bored with minute detail may wish to only scan the annotations of Chapter 2, Parts 1 and 2. The two most logical changes in the Constitution are at the end of Chapter 2 (Part 3) with further modifications consolidated at the end of Chapter 4 (Part 3). Another fix at the end of Chapter 5 limits corporations and is likely to be the most controversial. The proposals of the elite are in Chapter 6 while Chapter 7 covers a detailed convention plan, an important concept. Seven appendices are included as background and supporting information with Appendix 4 relating a long list of possible convention material called Tea Party bullets.

# CHAPTER ONE

## ONGOING PROBLEMS WITH THE CONSTITUTION

This chapter is broken down into sections chronologically to show some of the basic problems with the U.S. Constitution. Several of these criticisms have been ongoing ever since the original debate in 1787 at the convention in Philadelphia. It is assumed here that the reader has some familiarity with the Constitution. If you do not, it is best to review Chapter 2, Part 1, before you continue with the sections below.

1.  Arguments during the original debate

2.  The Ratification reasoning

3.  Civil War and Reconstruction

4.  President Wilson

5.  Modern day discussions

Some of the original problems were resolved, or partially fixed, by the amendment process provided in Article V of the Constitution. Principal among these were:

1.  Amendments I through X, The Bill of Rights

2.  Amendment XIII, Abolition of Slavery

3.  Amendment XIV, Reconstruction limits on States

4.  Amendments XV, XXIV, and XXVI; Suffrage

5.  Amendment XVI, Income Tax

6.  The remainder of the twenty-seven Amendments, while important, are mostly administrative in nature.


It is not possible to discuss all the complaints and criticisms concerning the Constitution in one short book. The major problems still under scrutiny, and limited to the areas noted above, will be covered in this chapter. Culture changes since 1787 are shown in Appendix 1 and an extensive list of problematic subjects (Tea Party bullets) are given in Appendix 4.

## PART ONE:  THE ORIGINAL DEBATE AT PHILADELPHIA

During the four months of debate (29 May to 17 Sept 1787) the Framers did an excellent job of considering just about every facet of modern government.  They used multiple examples available from historic civilizations and political philosophy; from Greece, to Rome, to European monarchies; and from Plato, to Cato, to Montesquieu and Locke.

Nevertheless, discord was common for even the Founders realized the Constitution did have, and would have, faults.  Three of the frequent dissenters were the delegates that "did not sign" the document, they were; Elbridge Gerry (a Massachusetts merchant), Colonel George Mason (a Virginia planter, soldier) and Edmund Randolph (a Virginia lawyer).  All three desired a follow-on second convention after further input from the States and the people.

Only a few of the naughty three's objections will be discussed in this section.[1]  The complaints chosen are some of those that are still valid today.  Of course many of the feared problems never materialized (e.g., the prognosis of monarchy or a tyrannical aristocracy), and others have been corrected through the amendment process (e.g., personal rights by the Bill of Rights and slavery by Amendments 13, 14, and 15 etc.)

One major objection by Mr. Gerry was the Judiciary appointment by the executive. To the present day this continues to sway reaction by the Senate in confirmations and by the people because of feared political bias by the chosen Supreme Court Judges.

---

[1] Ketcham, Ralph, ed., *The Anti-Federalist Papers,* Signet Classic, 2003, 171-175

Mr. Gerry also had problems with the duration and re-elect ability of the Senate. In modern parlance this is a term limit, which is a frequent concern in the 21st century. He was fearful of monopolies as well. An item never mentioned in the Constitution.

Another ongoing problem to which Mr. Randolph objected was the small number of representatives in comparison to population (at one to 30,000). What might he think today at one per approximately 600,000? Mr. Randolph was also against the "necessary and proper clause" (see Appendix 2) as well as unqualified pardons by the executive.

Colonel Mason's main objection was the lack of a Bill of Rights that was basically corrected with the first ten amendments. But that wasn't all, he also believed the Senate had too much power, that the executive should have a Council, and that the importation of slaves should not be allowed for another twenty years.

Even the father of the Constitution, Mr. Madison, was against the selection method and size of the Senate. He believed it to be un-republican and gave the minority a way to negative the majority. The situation remains to this day.

## PART TWO: THE RATIFICATION PERIOD

Ratification of the Constitution was assured by June 1788 with New Hampshire's approval. However, without ratification by the remaining large states, Virginia and New York, the system wasn't likely to function. Thankfully, these two states did ratify, but only after arming their delegations with numerous proposed amendments from the anti-federalists, which were in the majority in both states.

Virginia's most eloquent anti-federalist was Patrick Henry. He spoke for two days in June 1788 against the proposed Constitution. His concerns were among the forty amendments proposed by the Virginia ratification convention. Twenty of these were about personal rights, and generally satisfied by the Bill of Rights later adopted and ratified. The remaining twenty included items such as: [2]

1. Direct taxes.
2. Insufficient House representatives.
3. Commercial treaty approval.

New York, the eleventh state to ratify, was among the several States offering part of the total two hundred amendments submitted to Congress. These were later consolidated into about seventy-five to avoid duplication.[3] New York's Governor Clinton was an ardent anti-federalist. A political ally, writing under the synonym "Brutus," wrote essays reflecting the ideas and concerns of the New York anti-federalists.[4] Among his worries were:

1. The "necessary and proper clause," giving the national government too much absolute and uncontrollable power.
2. The authority to contract debts at the legislature's discretion.
3. The legislature to determine the definition of "general welfare."
4. The power to lay and collect taxes diluting the States' ability to do so.
5. Power distribution between States and national government not well defined.
6. The new union is not of the States, but of all the people.

---

[2] Labunski, Richard, *James Madison,* Oxford Univ. Press, 2006, 114
[3] Ibid., 199
[4] Ketcham, 271-307

7. The Supreme Court will extend central power by general construction of the Constitution and the States will loose power.

8. The preamble abolishes State power.

9. The eighth section of Article one, expressly or by implication, extends to almost everything.

10. There is no control of the Judiciary for errors in judgment.

We see that with only summarizing objections by two of the major ratifying states, there continued to be a plethora of problems with the Constitution at this historical stage.

## PART THREE: CIVIL WAR AND RECONSTRUCTION

There were three amendments ratified after the Civil War during the Reconstruction period. Together they prohibited slavery, provided the standards of civil rights, increased federal authority and provided suffrage for black men. Two of these, the thirteenth and the fifteenth, were fairly straightforward and did not create great controversy. The fourteenth however was in Justice Rehnquist's words, full of "fuzzy generalities."[5]

The 13th Amendment: It should be remembered that the North's official aim of the Civil War, that started in April of 1861, was to preserve the Union. Lincoln's Emancipation Proclamation, freeing the slaves, wasn't issued until the first day of 1863. To further enforce and support the Emancipation, the 13th Amendment was designed to prohibit slavery and involuntary servitude. Congress passed it in January 1865. This occurred before the war concluded in April 1865 with Lee's surrender at Appomattox Court House. By December 1865 the amendment was ratified.

Even though intended to establish personal liberties, both the Courts and Congress took a fairly narrow interpretation of the amendment allowing States to regulate civil rights and discriminate with "Black Codes." This failure of the Southern States to take a reasonable view in the enforcement of the 13th Amendment would lead to further Amendments.

---

[5] Rehnquist, William H., *The Supreme Court,* Alfred A. Knopf, 2004, 95

The 15th Amendment:  Saving the most controversial for last, a short coverage of the fifteenth Amendment seems appropriate before covering the lengthy fourteenth. The 15th Amendment provides suffrage for all races, but not women.  It passed Congress in March 1869 and was ratified in 1870.  With only the Reconstruction Act of 1867 holding the ex-Confederate States to forced black suffrage, the Republican controlled Congress feared the law might be insecure without an Amendment.    The Amendment was later used by the Supreme Court to prevent racial gerrymandering and literacy tests.

The 14th Amendment:  The fourteenth Amendment is by far the most controversial of all the Amendments and whole books[6] have been written about this single amendment. In contrast to most other amendments that are virtually single issue, the 14th has multiple topics in section one.  For discussion purposes these topics are normally broken out by the separate clauses as they appear in the text. The topics are:  1) Citizenship, 2) State Action, 3) Privileges or Immunities, 4) Due Process, and 5) Equal Protection. Sections two, three and four of the 14th are more Reconstruction specific and are of minor consequence today (mid 2010).  Section five is called the "enforcement clause," and is a duplicate of section two of the 13th Amendment. It was inserted again specifically to re-emphasize the power granted to Congress to write enforcement laws, even though this power was previously granted in Article I, section 8 of the basic constitution.

The five clauses in section one of the 14th Amendment cause by far the most litigation of any amendment.  *The Heritage Guide to the Constitution*[7] for example lists 93 Supreme Court (the Court) cases concerning the amendment. The First Amendment comes in a distant second place at 68 significant cases.[8] Section one is responsible for most of the liberal social changes in our law.  Because of the complexity, the associated Court cases are also the most reversed.  This did not happen immediately after ratification and in fact most of the implied, substantive changes did not occur until after World War II.  That is, the Court's interpretation of the 14th Amendment was in the originalist, strict construction, and State's rights mode for several decades and the States, both North and

---

[6] Nelson, William E., *The Fourteenth Amendment*, Harvard Univ. Press, 1988.
[7] Messe, Edwin III, Ed. Chair, *The Heritage Guide to the Constitution,* Regency, 2005, 386-409
[8] Ibid, 302-318

South, were generally allowed to make their own rules, even though the new federally enforceable civil rights amendments had been established. One could call this holdover States' rights era the "segregation" or "separate but equal" time period.

Then came a period in which the Court began to flex its muscle and defining State law limits more as the Congress had originally intended. During this mid-term era from about 1900 until after World War II the Court flip-flopped back and forth between originalist civil rights determinations and more social and political rulings. After the Second World War, rulings became much more liberal.

So what's the problem? The problem is that the 14th Amendment is too flexible and ill defined. The Court cannot be expected to strictly interpret a poorly worded amendment without being accused of making law on their own. Modern conservatives have yet to admit to this problem in a serious manner.

Most Constitution clauses are listed in Appendix 2 with some discussion mini briefs. Clause by clause questions and problems for section one of the 14th Amendment arc as follows:

1. Citizenship:
   a) American Indians and jurisdiction
   b) Illegal aliens born in the United States
2. State Action:
   a) The Court changed its rulings twice between 1883, 1966, and 2000.
   b) State action or its derivatives versus individual regulation is still not resolved.
3. Privileges or Immunities:
   a) No good definition
   b) Substantive natural rights dictum of 1823 was consistent with the 1866 Civil Rights Act but was changed and negated by the *Slaughter-House* cases of 1873. This effectively stopped use of the clause.

4. Due Process:

   a) A duplication of the 5th Amendment.

   b) Frequently disputed since the Framers' intentions were unclear.

   c) Narrow procedure process meaning is now lost in substantive portions.

   d) Used in contract disputes, then reversed and re-reversed.

   e) Extended to the concept of privacy, approving abortion and homosexuality, but not assisted suicide.

   f) Selectively incorporated the Bill of Rights into State law.

5. Equal Protection:

   a) Frequently litigated and the debate of original understanding continues.

   b) The word "equally" is not well defined. Does it mean "same?"

   c) Most laws require some classifications and distinctions. Court methods are unclear.

   d) Is a tiered system of standards the best?

   e) Affirmative-action quota questions remain.

Why can't we call this the preverbal bucket-of-worms that it truly is. The 14th Amendment was intended as a civil rights document for slaves to incorporate the 1866 Civil Rights Act and did not include political and social concepts. The result was segregation until the Court began substantive interpretations. The bottom line is that there is no return to the originalist conservative mode without Constitutional reform.

Finally, we should not leave the Reconstruction era without mentioning Walter Bagehot (an English banker turned journalist) who wrote a book in 1867 called *The English Constitution*.[9] One basic thesis was that his English government was better than the U.S. government and he frequently compared the two. The premise was that the executive (Prime Minister and Cabinet) and the legislature (House of Commons) worked closely together to advantage and that in addition the legislature could remove the Prime Minister at will and that the Prime Minister could similarly dissolve the House if things

---

[9] Bagehot, Walter, *The English Constitution,* reprint by Cornell Univ. Press, 1971

were not getting accomplished. Since both the executive and the legislature in the U.S. are elected for fixed terms and are not intermingled, this perceived advantage to representative government in the United States is not possible. Bagehot's theories and logic were referenced repeatedly by Woodrow Wilson in his speeches and writings several decades later and will be covered further in the next section.

**PART FOUR:  WOODROW WILSON**

Thomas Woodrow Wilson is probably more famous as a political scientist than as President of the United States (1913-1921). He is the only Ph.D. to become President, but was not a nerd per se, since he did play golf and coach football.[10] Born in 1856, he grew up in the South after the Civil War. In his day he was called a progressive liberal. By today's standards he would be considered a moderate conservative, and, as with many liberals, he became more conservative as time progressed.

Wilson's academic accomplishments before becoming President were several books and articles about the problems with our government and our Constitution. His first major work, *Congressional Government*,[11] was written in 1883 and 1884 for his Ph.D. dissertation. Multiple additions have since been published. In the context of the post Civil War period, Wilson worried that the President was too weak and the Congress too strong. He thought the Constitution was severely defective and needed to be made over to resemble the British "parliamentary system." Using Walter Bagehot's book about the so-called "unwritten" English Constitution as a guide, Wilson criticized our "presidential system" with congressional committees as inefficient and unworkable.

A few assertions (paraphrased or quoted) from *Congressional Government* are given here to show Wilson's early points of view. Page numbers refer to the referenced addition.

---

[10]  Durant, John & Alice, *Pictorial History of American Presidents,* A.S. Barnes and Co., N.Y., 1955, 224+
[11]  Wilson, Woodrow, *Congressional Government*, Riverside Press, Houghton Mifflin Co., 1885, N.Y., Referenced addition: Dover Publications, 2006, N.Y.

1. Wilson was one of the first to call for a "living system" of government. p19 (Later called his Darwinian approach.)

2. It is absolutely necessary to have financial administration in the hands of a few highly trained and skillful men acting subject to strict responsibility, which our committee system does not allow. p102

3. Multiple committees handle expenditures and the currency and this is too complex. p103

4. An immense budget is rushed through without discussion in a week or ten days no matter which party is in power. No other nation attempts such a thing. p133

5. We are forced to amend the Constitution without constitutionally amending it. The process is slow and cumbersome. p163

6. The play of civil institutions should not alter the play of economic forces. Capital is the breath of life to Congress. p194

7. Our extra-constitutional party convention constitutes the only machinery for executive control. p195

8. Our Constitution puts the power to make laws and control expenditures with Congress, but by separating it from the Executive, it deprives Congress of complete authority. p203

9. Editors direct public opinion, and Congressmen obey it, except when an election is near. Both conservative and liberal editors should report both sides of a story. p207-208

10. The more open-eyed we become to the defects of our Constitution the sooner we will find the courage of conviction and the expedients to make self-government straight forward with clear responsibility, and approach the common sense ideals of the Founders. p215

Wilson's second major work, *Constitutional Government*,[12] was basically an update of his earlier *Congressional Government*. Although still convinced the parliamentary system more efficient than ours, he changed his mind about executive power and the possibilities of changing the Constitution. Since Wilson was not elected President until

---

[12] Wilson, Woodrow, *Constitutional Government in the United States*, Columbia Univ. Press, 1908
Referenced copy: Transition Publications, New Brunswick, 2006, w/intro by Sidney A. Pearson Jr., 2002

1912 he was still a "literary politician" at the writing of the lectures he used in this newer book in 1907. While some of his ideas and pronouncements turned out to be in error, one cannot negate his contribution to political science. Wilson continued to use Bagehot, Hegel, Tocqueville, Rousseau and others for background information. But two major things had changed. One, the importance of the President was reasserted by the advent of the Spanish American War, and second, Wilson decided the Constitution would be too difficult to change and his theories needed to be modified to work within the present system. As before, paraphrased and quoted items from *Constitutional Government* are used below to give a flavor of his interest and contributions in constitutional study.

1. The Constitution does not have to be written and has to be adapted to interests of the people and maintenance of individual liberty. p2

2. Political liberty is the right of those who are governed to adjust government to their own needs and interests—this is the philosophy of constitutional government. p4

3. The theory of English and American law is that no man must look to have the government take care of him, but that every man must take care of himself. p19

4. Essential elements and institutions should include an assembly representing the community; a body to control, restrain and criticize government. p23

5. Nothing but a community of common interests can have a constitution. p25

6. The legislature has a tendency to enact impracticable laws, since they don't have to put them into execution and can put any blame on the Executive. p39

7. In a parliamentary system the people's leaders majority suggest, enact and then execute the laws. p40

8. In our system only one man is the choice of all the people and he doesn't lead Congress. Men who are "not" national leaders guide our Congress. p40

9. Self-government is not mere institutions but a form of character following long discipline, habit of order, and reverence of law and political maturity. All this takes time. You cannot "give" self-government. p52 (In the Philippines it took about 12 years, from 1934 to 1946.)

10. At the time of the founding, the Whig party in England was in a struggle to curb and regulate power of the Crown. Our revolution leaders held Whig doctrine. These influences sparked the checks and balances theories. p198+

11. Party organizations exist quite independent of the executive and legislature and are "far" from democratic. p203

12. We have kept government in a workable combination by outside pressure of a closely-knit party, a body with no constitutional cleavages and free to get into legislative functions through personnel control. p205

13. The three Federal branches are not merged or even drawn into organic cooperation, but balanced against each other, interdependent but disassociated, with no common authority. p205

14. Local parties are indispensable to party discipline and rewards and party machinery are essential to keep several segments or factions together. p209

15. Only in the U.S. are parties a direct distinct authority outside formal government dictating what Congress will undertake and the administration address. p211

16. Party control limits the guise of self-government to a farce. p214

17. Local bosses often control selection of Congressional members. p214

18. We need to make our legislature and executive the real coordinated body politic instead of parties, thereby requiring fewer checks and balances. p221

19. The Constitution needs constant revitalization. p222

Finally, a summary of Woodrow's tenure as President is of interest. Could he practice what he had been preaching? The information for this time frame was derived primarily from *The President as Statesman, Woodrow Wilson and the Constitution*[13] as well as various American history books.

Once Mr. Wilson became President in March 1913 he instigated his executive/congressional buddy-buddy theory and along with a Democrat Congress was initially quite successful. His "New Freedom" programs of tariff reform, establishment

---

[13] Stid, Daniel D., *The President as Statesman*, Univ. Press of Kansas, 1998.

of the Federal Reserve System plus the Federal Trade Commission, and anti-trust legislation, should be placed on the positive side of his ledger. Added to this list can be: authorization of the Coast Guard, keeping the German surrogates out of Mexico, pursuing Poncho Villa, opening the Panama Canal, establishing the National Guard, recognizing the importance of air power, and the winning of World War I. He also is recognized for his principled party platforms, recommendations for presidential primaries, criticizing the political influence of foreigners, supporting States' rights on prohibition, passionate support of the League of Nations, and the establishment of the routine press conference.

In the more negative category were: his early reluctance to get into the war, even after numerous German U-boat attacks and deaths of U.S. citizens; initial disapproval of woman's suffrage; indifference to racial matters; starting a federal farm program; beginning aid to education; a general acceleration of big government; allowing a poor peace treaty, which some historians say helped to start World War II; and finally, not resigning after three strokes, thus leaving his second wife to be the pseudo first female President of the United States.

On Wilson's change-your-mind flip-flop register would be: changing support from a parliamentary system back to the presidential system of the Founders; giving up on Constitutional Amendments to working within the Constitution; moving from a neutral pacifist position to get reelected to vigorously supporting the war; letting the States handle women's suffrage at first to later favoring the 19th Amendment; being adamantly against secret caucuses and the spoils system to tolerating them as politically necessary; to oscillating between a non-written constitution theory to the need for a definite formulated and understood document; from chastising the party system to recognizing its favorable contributions; and after vowing to appoint only progressives to the cabinet and other appointments, to backing down in the face of spoils system pressure from his own Democrat party. The election of a questionably qualified President in 2008 and the resulting mid-term House results in 2010 should again raise Wilson's question as to whether the parliamentary system is superior to our presidential system.

This rather extensive section on Woodrow Wilson is to give the reader important background information on the first very serious attempt by an high-powered academic and politician to access what might be done to improve the efficiency of our government. We will now skip forward to semi-recent literary suggestions on how to solve some of our problems using Constitutional changes.

# CHAPTER 1: PART 5   FULL SCALE REWRITES

Part 5 contains two sections.  Beginning with older rewrites of the 1970s in Part 5A and then five more recent books with multiple suggestions in Part 5B, detailed comparisons are made of the various Constitution reforms using tables.

## PART 5A:  TUGWELL and BALDWIN

At least two authors took up the task of completely rewriting the Constitution in the early 1970s.  Rexford Guy Tugwell working with, and as a Senior Fellow, in the Center for the Study of Democratic Institutions[14] in the late 1960s rewrote the entire Constitution after some thirty-seven drafts and published it in 1970.  Tugwell had a long career in academia and government service. He was part of President F. D. Roosevelt's "brain trust" and is best labeled as a liberal progressive.  In approximately 1976 he wrote an additional and thoughtful book[15] about the Constitution supporting but not mentioning his original work.  A summary quote from this book helps in understanding his work:

> But amendments have been few and alteration by implication has been frequent; consequently they offer the most serious instances.  Consider, for example, the erection of a shaky structure on the equal protection clause of the fourteenth amendment or the decision that another clause turns corporations into persons.  Still more serious, there are the implications drawn from the original constitution, called attention to in this essay:  executive budgeting; congressional oversight of the executive; presidential monopolizing of legislative initiative; the invention of "emergency" and its uses for expanding the powers of the commander-in-chief; the establishment by the Court of judicial supremacy; the strained meaning of concurrent sovereignty—all these and more. ...   By now the government rests on far too thin a constitutional base.  That base needs thorough—not piecemeal—reconsideration.[16]

A second author, Leland D. Baldwin, also wrote a completely reworked Constitution[17] in 1972.  A retired professor of history from the University of

---

[14] R. G. Tugwell, *Model for a New Constitution,* Center For The Study Of Democratic Institutions, Santa Barbara, CA and James E. Freel & Associates, Palo Alto, CA, 1970.

[15] R. G. Tugwell, *The Compromising of the Constitution,* University of Notre Dame Press, Notre Dame, IN, date not given but approximately 1976.

[16] Ibid, p. 178.

[17] L. D. Baldwin, *Reframing the Constitution,* American Bibliographical Center—Clio Press, Santa Barbara, CA; Oxford, England, 1972.

Pittsburgh, Professor Baldwin also had a liberal leaning, although somewhat less than Mr. Tugwell. The "essential thesis"[18] of Baldwin's book is:

1.  To make provisions in the Constitution for guardians of the public welfare with greater legislative and administrative flexibility.

2.  To give the electorate more power to force the government to take notice of the public will.

To accomplish his thesis some of his most basic proposals were:[19]

1.  That State power is no longer viable and State sovereignty needs to be modified.

2.  For Congress to become a unicameral body which includes the President.

3.  That Constitutional provisions for organization of parties, the selection of candidates, the holding of conventions, and the governing and financing of campaigns—all come under the general supervision of a reconstructed Senate.

4.  To solve the rule of majority with a handpicked Senate of thoughtful people.

Baldwin goes on to warn us that without these solutions our social conditions will disintegrate until: "God save us! – A leader will emerge who will do for the United States what Caesar did for Rome, Cromwell for England, and Napoleon for France."[20]

Without going into minute detail a comparison of these two authors is given next along with their 1787 Constitution relationship. The tabular form includes major topics and reference page numbers.

---

[18]  Ibid, p; xii.
[19]  Ibid, p. xii, xiii.
[20]  Ibid, p. xiv.

# CHAPTER 1: PART 5A  TABLE 1  COMPARISONS

| Terms | 1787 Const. | Tugwell, 1970 | Baldwin, 1972 |
|---|---|---|---|
| President | 4 yrs, 2 terms max (Art VI, 3.1; Amendment 22) | 9 yr, one term with 3 yr possible rejection (p56) | 5 yrs, no term limit, Congress majority can remove (p125) |
| House | 2 yrs, no term limit (Art I, 2) | N/A | Unicameral, 5 yrs unless dissolved (p119). Extra appointments possible (p123). |
| Senate | 6 yrs, no term limit (Art I, 3) | Life, President appointment or special experience (p61, 62) | Life, integrated with judiciary (p128). |
| Senate Power | Make laws, Approve appointments and treaties, Try impeachments (Art I, 3,7; Art II, 2) | Same as 1787 plus approves IG, plans and elects Overseer (p48,54,64). Approves foreign deployments (p58). Can suspend operations of Republics (previously States)(p47). May remove Pres. with 2/3 vote (p59). May relieve Principle (Chief) Justice (p76). Final say on Const. Interpretation (p78). | Integrated with judiciary. Senate is highest court (p128). Chief Justice presides over and is elected by Senate (p133). Senate makes property rules and sets its own budget (p133). Chief may dissolve Congress (p134). |

|  | 1787 Const. | Tugwell | Baldwin |
|---|---|---|---|
| Judiciary | Membership and system set by Congress (Art I, 8,9 & Art III, 1). Prime for Const., ex-state and appellate cases (Art III, 2). | Have a Council, Assembly and lots of special courts (p74). Council may impeach legislators with trial by Highest court (p86). Exception for outside income (p83). May appraise property and institute draft (p70). May approve mergers (p73). Suggests Const. Amendments (p76). Judges decide if jury required (76). | Senate is the highest court (p128). Chief Justice presides over Senate (p133). Chief appoints court members (p133). Chief may dissolve Congress with 2/3 Senate approval (p134). No jury except for murder or treason (p141). |
| Amendment Methods | Congress may propose by 2/3 votes, or 2/3 of States can call for convention. Ratification by 3/4 States. (Art. V). | Council suggests (p76). If Senate and President approve sent to electorate. If not disapproved by majority of electorate becomes law (p86). | Either Congress or Senate may propose by 2/3 votes and be approved by ¾ of State legislatures or by majority of electorate (p141). Any State may propose and if ½ States agree it goes to national vote. A convention can be called by 2/3 of both houses and a revision has 5 yrs to be approved by States and electorate. Any State, with 2/3 of others, can call a convention with revisions approved by the people (142). |
| Campaign Finance | N/A | No private or candidate contributions (51). Public financing above 2% of vote (p107, 114). | Senate controls by law (p135). |
| Number of States | Unlimited (Art IV, 3.1) | Commission sets new boundaries with minimum of 5% of population. Called Republics (p45). | Sixteen regional areas restructured into new States (p61). |

There are two more full-scale changes published in article rather than book form. John R. Vile summarized these in his excellent reference in 1991.[21] His book is given special attention in Chapter 6.

The first was by Charles Coleman in 1938.[22] Coleman, I found out after my original research work, made some similar proposals as this author, such as eliminating obsolete provisions, incorporating amendments, etc. His proposal is the first known complete rewritten draft. He was also in favor of longer terms for Congress, elimination of the Vice President, regulation of corporations and labor, easier ratification of amendments and other interesting ideas. Vile considered him a conservative and wondered why later scholars did not expand or respond to some of his suggestions.

Another draft-type article was written by Jeremy M. Miller 1987,[23] well after the books by Tugwell and Baldwin covered above. He surmised that the 200-year centennial was a good time to revisit the subject. Among his proposals were a balanced budget, prohibitions against paternalism, and paying more attention to ethics, natural law, religion and smaller government to name a few. Miller was the only one to suggest a lottery to balance the budget and to have a minimum and maximum income tax. He also recommended modernizing the vocabulary, the topic of the next chapter and Chapter 3.

---

[21] Vile, John R., *Rewriting the U.S. Constitution,* Praeger Publishers, 1991.
[22] Coleman, Charles, "The Constitution Up to Date," National Council of Social Studies Bulletin no.10, Cambridge, Mass. 1938.
[23] Miller, Jeremy M., "It's Time for a New Constitution," Southwestern Univ. Law Review 17, 1987, 207+.

# CHAPTER 1:  PART 5B

# MORE RECOMMENDATIONS FOR IMPROVEMENT

In this part authors who have made serious recommendations for improving the Constitution are reviewed.  The only drawback is that they give few specifics on how one might format and implement their suggestions and proposals, except in general to say we need a convention for that purpose.  Chapter 7 addresses the convention problem.

Five references are considered in some detail with their publishing dates ranging from 1974 to 2007.  This is certainly not all of the recent literature on the subject.  Selections (author's bias) were made of those with a more moderate leaning as opposed to those, which were deemed overly liberal.  Books with limited or single subject matter were also rejected.  For example, Judge Napolitano's scary and interesting work[24] on how the government breaks its own laws, covers primarily just the courts, the Justice Department and local law enforcement.  It was therefore not included in the analysis.

Comparing the five references reveals common threads.  Not that the author agrees with all of them, but some make enough sense that the general public would probably concur with a few of their recommendations.

Generalized comments for each book are given first, followed by a comparison table similar to Part 5A. This makes it easier for the reader to see areas of consensus.

## BOOK # 1:  *A NEW CONSTITUTION NOW*  (1942/1974)

Henry Hazlitt's[25] reference will be considered first.  Hazlitt was an economic journalist and literary editor who worked primarily in New York.  He would be considered a moderate conservative by today's standards in contrast to the other authors exposed here.  His book is really two books, written first in 1942 because of concern

---

[24] Napolitano, Andrew P., *Constitutional Chaos,* Nelson Current, Nashville TN, 2004.
[25] Hazlitt, Henry, *A New Constitution Now,* Arlington House, 1974.

about the inefficiencies of our government which might result in losing World War II, and secondly in 1974 because of the Watergate scandal.

Much the same as Woodrow Wilson, Hazlitt believed the parliamentary system vastly superior to our presidential system because the leadership is held more responsible and removable on short notice. He was a great believer in the principle of "concentration of responsibility." At the same time he stressed that even parliamentary governments needed deliberate restrictions and that, similar to Fredrick Hayek,[26] central economic planning would lead to moral decay and even dictatorship. That is, small government is best, and efficient responsible government is essential to prevent fatal failure in time of war or during rampant inflation. He feared the presidential system balance of power only a paper theory resting near instability, like on the point of a pin, always in crisis and leaning toward executive dictatorship. Hazlitt's book title, not changed in the 32 years between rewrites, summarizes his position--we need "A New Constitution Now."

## BOOK # 2: *THE COMMITTEE ON THE CONSTITUTIONAL SYSTEM* (1982--85)

This reference is a gathering of essays compiled together as "*Reforming American Government.*"[28] It is an excellent source about the positive and negative aspects of our Constitution. A forty-one board of directors participated over a three-year period starting in 1982. The authors of the various articles and proposals came from a variety of fields, including previous Senators, Congressmen, State Governors, Cabinet secretaries, academics, journalists, etc.

Essay number twelve defines the problem as the committee saw it emphasizing that technology has changed the world and our citizens have lost confidence in our leaders and institutions. They stress that the "balance of power" is outdated and produces poor policies and foreign leader confusion.

---

[26] Hayek, Friedrich A., *The Road To Serfdom,* University of Chicago Press, 1944.
[28] Robinson, Donald L. (editor), *Reforming American Government, The Bicentennial Papers of the Committee on the Constitutional system, Westview Press, Boulder CO, 1985.*

On a positive note, the committee did propose twelve Amendments in semi-constitutional format and discussed their pros and cons. Subjects covered were: changing office terms, team tickets, bonus Congressional seats for the President's party, mixing legislators with the executive, dissolution of government, legislative vetoes, referendums, line item vetoes, and reduced treaty ratification requirements.

Several other topics were covered in the essays including: campaign finance, party problems, television, budgets, impeachment, and constitutional conventions, for example. Even foreign constitutions were compared.

Unfortunately, no votes appear to have been taken by the committee members on the Amendments proposed; perhaps because they were somewhat reluctant to stick their necks out to criticism. Instead, they stressed an overall theme of trying to open-up the subject of Constitution revision for further discussion. To that end they may be at least partially successful, if this author's work attracts a reasonable group of readers.

## Book # 3: *CONSTITUTION REFORM and EFFECTIVE GOVERNMENT* (1992)

James L. Sundquist wrote this reference while a senior fellow at the Brookings Institution. He is the author of several books about the government and this one[29] is among his best. The previous reference (#2) also contains three of his essays.

His work is well done with lots of facts and good ideas. Unfortunately, his anti-conservative and pro Democrat ideology shows,[30] not perhaps as a flaming liberal, but certainly as a moderate one, with his unabashed approval of universal health care and low-income housing (a serious contributor to the 2008/2010 recession).

Sunquist's biggest fears were a paralysis in foreign policy in time of crisis and a budget out of control (which came true in 2008/2010). In my opinion the aircraft terrorist

---

[29] Sundquist, James L., *Constitutional Reform and Effective Government,* The Brookings Institution, Washington DC, revised 1992 from 1986.
[30] Ibid, pp. 7 & 13.

crisis of 11 September 2001 was actually handled without too much difficulty as the Congress passed power to the executive as it often does under such conditions. The serious failure in that case was poor intelligence, not the administration reaction.

In addition to the two serious concerns above, nine other items[31] are suggested as a series of amendments and include: 1) A common slate of candidates from each party to be voted on as a team; 2) Lengthening of the terms of office for both Houses; 3) Changes in the method of selecting the President; 4) Some way to call a special election when the government fails; 5) Allowing Congress members to work in the executive branch; 6) A line item anti-pork executive power with override provisions; 7) A limited legislative two-house veto; 8) Updated war power provisions; and 9) A reduced treaty vote requirement using both Houses.

Several more of his suggestions, such as public campaign financing, new party rules, etc., were cased as possible statutory changes. But for all his reasonable ideas, Mr. Sundquist was not very upbeat about anything really getting done. None of his proposed amendments are formatted for direct Constitutional inclusion. He fears convention runaway, the lack of popular interest in institutional change, and the ease with which amendments may be blocked, by well lobbied congresspersons, given that only a small percentage of votes can block them in either House of Congress, or the State legislative houses. See Chapter 7 for a solution to this problem.

## Book # 4: *OUR UNDEMOCRATIC CONSTITUTION (2006)*

Sanford Levinson[32] who is a law academic and author with multiple publications wrote reference number four. As one might expect, his work leans to the liberal side.

Among his concerns about the Constitution are:

1. A Senate representation not based on population.

2. Excessive Presidential veto power.

---

[31] Ibid, pp. 323-324
[32] Levinson, Sanford, *Our Undemocratic Constitution,* Oxford University Press, 2006.

3. A major fear of a terrorist attack that will desecrate the House of Representatives with no way to replace their numbers quickly.

4. Serious problems with the Presidential election and the Electoral College.

5. Doubts about judicial life tenure.

6. Office qualifications, which are too stringent.

7. The difficult amendment process.

Professor Levinson makes no specific amendment proposals but does spend several pages promoting the convention process. In contrast to other authors he believes liberals to be more fearful of a runaway convention than conservatives. My research tends to indicate just the opposite in that conservatives are usually the strict constructionists.

Despite Levinson's liberal tendencies, his book is well written and has many logical arguments about needed revisions to our Constitution. And, like many other authors on the subject, he primarily promotes more discussion.

## BOOK # 5: *A MORE PERFECT CONSTITUTION (2007)*

This final modern reference[33] was written in 2007 by Larry J. Sabato, the director of the Center for Politics at the University of Virginia. A distinguished professor and the recipient of a Ph.D. from Oxford University, he has written several books about politics and appears on Fox TV frequently. More middle of the road than most academics, Professor Sabato is not afraid of the right leaning media such as Fox news, and quotes Thomas Jefferson as one of his heroes. There were, of course, no liberals at the founding in this author's opinion.

Since Doctor Sabato's work is the most recent, I'll attempt to directly address all 23 of his proposals[34] in a condensed format. Comments are in parentheses.

---

[33] Sabato, Larry J. *A More Perfect Constitution 23 Proposals to Revitalize Our Constitution and Make America a* Fairer *Country,* Walker & Company, New York, 2007.
[34] Ibid, p. 225.

## Congress:

1. Several more Senate seats for larger States and D.C. (This would reduce small State power and confuse the representative tenant of the House. Note that one of the goals of Lex Ferenda is to foster changes that are fairly simple and straightforward.)

2. Appoint ex-Presidents and ex-Vice Presidents as "national" Senators. (Executives turn pretty gray during their terms and should be tired of politics. They might also meddle more in foreign affairs than they already do.)

3. Federal House redistricting. (States' job, but prohibiting irregular shapes could work.)

4. Lengthen House terms and elect the whole House and Senate at the same time as the President. (Agree with the first part, but not simultaneous elections. Staggered terms are essential for continuity.)

5. Increase House size to 1000 members. (Committees are already too large and fail to get their work accomplished. Auxiliary representatives back home might help.)

6. Term limits. (Absolutely—most corruption in later terms.)

7. Balanced budget (Yes—out of control, both parties.)

8. Disaster continuity. (Long overdue.)

## Presidency:

9. Six-year term with extension referendum. (Too complicated/expensive.)

10. Limit war powers. (See Chapter 4---The President is clearly responsible for defense of the nation and must have the corresponding flexibility. The Congress can declare war and control expenditures on war if it so desires. Professor Sabato's anti-war stance is a bit troublesome here.)

11. Line item veto. (O.K.---with override limits.)

12. Allow aliens to be President if a U.S. citizen for 20 years. (We have plenty of talented natural-born citizens. Doesn't pass the necessary test.)

## Federal Courts:

13. Fifteen-year nonrenewable terms for Federal judges. (The age restriction of the next item seems sufficient)

14. Age limit for Federal judges set by Congress. (Could be in the Constitution to strengthen separation of powers. Limit to a few years less than the average insurance company longevity age, but keep the "good behavior" requirement.)

15. Expand the Supreme Court to twelve. (Management literature often uses seven as the ideal committee size and an odd number is important to break ties.)

16. Cost-of-living salary increases, (O.K.---Key to a percentage of GDP.)

## Politics:

17. A separate Constitutional Article to cover political systems and parties. (OK--But details would be variable and very difficult to work out.)

18. Establish a regional lottery for Presidential nominating schedule, and limit the time frame. (Yes--Good idea.)

19. More Electors from larger States with "unit-voting" elimination. (How many more Electors without diluting small State power?)

20. Establish reasonable limits on campaign expenditures and use some public financing. (Overdue---Agree.)

21. Automatic voter registration. (I'm not convinced all citizens should have exactly the same rights in voting. If you don't take the trouble to register you probably are not very well informed. Sabato points out[35] that many citizens have little civic education or knowledge.)

## National Service:

22. Require two years government service from all citizens. (Generally agree.)

Constitutional Convention:

23. Call a Constitution Convention using the Article V State based method. (Agree, see my Chapter 7)

Many of Sabato's ideas have some previous history with the possible exception of National Service, which is a good idea. Two years of service for everyone may be a little long for such a large population but certainly some obligation and responsibility to insure

---

[35] Sabato, p.224.

our liberty and freedom seems reasonable. His second best idea is the lottery primary scheme, which shortens campaigns and gives better regional and State participation.

Sabato's work is the latest of the modern constitutional books thus far (2009) and is highly recommended reading because of his extensive notes and references plus a poll of public reaction. Although telephone based polls have accuracy problems, his poll[36] did show majority support for his proposals 4,6,10,13,14,18 and 20. The most important and in need of greater weight and attention are items 6,7,10,20 and 23.

With Sabato's book we are getting closer and closer to what needs to be done. As with other academics, however, Sabato believes more discussion and debate are necessary.[37] To that I must say "an emphatic no," more talk is wasting time! This topic has already been seriously discussed for at least two generations and really goes clear back to the founding with the anti-federalists. When will we actually do something? At some point we must graduate from discussion to consolidation of ideas and action beyond Tea Parties, sit-ins, and tractor-trips and before we get to pitchforks. The idea here is to avoid coming to pitchforks. But so far, rhetoric, learned articles and books have not solved the problem. Congress is not likely to act because changes will reduce their power. The State Governors, State legislators, or the public must react soon, in a positive fashion, or more drastic steps by irate citizens will surely be forthcoming. The action necessary is a second Constitution convention, and soon.

---

[36] Ibid, p.182.
[37] Ibid, p.229

**CHAPTER 1  TABLE 2:   MODERN REFERENCE COMPARISON**

| Book # , Author | 1  Hazlitt | 2  CSS | 3  Sundquist | 4  Levinson | 5  Sabato |
|---|---|---|---|---|---|
| Change Terms | | | | | |
| President | Yes (25,108) | Yes (3,109,284) | No (172) | Yes (119) | Yes (84,226) |
| House | Yes (28) | Yes (104,149) | Yes (154,323) | No (65) | Yes (93,226) |
| Senate | No (114) | Yes (104,149) | Yes (163,323) | No (50) | Yes (95,226) |
| Increase Senate Power | No (114) | No (150,262) | No (312,324) | Yes (49,50) | No (23,225) |
| Increase Court Power | No (32,108) | N/A | N/A | No (123,124) | No (108,227) |
| Change Amend. Method | Yes (24,32) | Yes (273) | DNR (16,323) | Yes (21,165) | DNR (8,199,229) |
| Campaign Finance Reform | Yes (25) | Yes (30,102 107,120,122) | Yes (274) | DNR (29) | Yes (33,152 184,228) |
| Balanced Budget Reform | Yes (114,152) | Yes (106,109,164) | DNR (4,109 322,328) | DNR (26,36,45) | Yes (54,226) |

(  ) --Page numbers;  N/A---Not Addressed;    DNR--Discussed but No Recommendation

In the next chapter, changes are annotated to the basic Constitution and the Amendments and then incorporated into the present Constitution.  No content meaning changes are suggested until Chapter 3.

# CHAPTER TWO

# DELETIONS & AMENDMENT INCORPERATIONS

The first task is to bring the basic 1787 Constitution together into a more readable form by updating spelling and deleting the clauses that are no longer needed. For example, clauses used by the Framers/Founders to get the original document into physical operation. To make this process easier to understand, I have used Part 1 of this chapter to annotate the original document. In doing so, a few coded abbreviations have been used. The ancient capitalization has been retained for the most part to emphasize the historical importance of the original document. In general, clauses associated with the initial establishment, the Civil War reconstruction, or commonly repeated dialog, have been noted for deletion by *italics*. Original sections where present Amendment language should be inserted are also indicated by annotation. Sections to be changed are <u>underlined</u> and in brackets.

In Part 2, since some Amendments have been further amended, I have annotated the present (2010) outstanding Amendments for inclusion in the basic document. The Bill of Rights, in its entirety, is moved to the main body just after the preamble. The remaining amendments are given notations for incorporation into the main articles that cover congress, the executive, and the judiciary in such a way as to make them traceable by lawyers and judges, an important aspect of modernization. Below is a table showing roughly how and where the present Amendments were sifted into the main document.

Part 3 incorporates the annotated changes of Part 1 and Part 2 into the Constitution. Note that no meaning content or basic substance has been knowingly changed in this chapter. The results of this chapter could probably stand alone as a new Amendment.
In the next chapter some obviously needed wording and relative basic changes are considered.

To recap, this chapter includes the table of Amendment insertions below plus:

      Part 1: Annotates the original Constitution as it stands today (2010)
      Part 2: Annotates the present Amendments.
      Part 3: Incorporates these annotated changes into the Constitution.


## TABLE OF AMENDMENT INCORPERATIONS

Bill of Rights:      Inserted after preamble

Amendment XI:      Incorporated into Section 2, Article III

Amendment XII:     Incorporate in Section 1, Article II

Amendment XIII:    Incorporate in Section 2, Article VI

Amendment XIV:   Section 1: Added to Section 2, Article IV
                 Section 2: Changes part of Section 2, Article I
                 Section 3: Add to Section 3, Article III
                 Section 4: Add after first sentence of Article VI

Amendment XV:    Add after sentence one of Section 2, Article IV

Amendment XVI:   Incorporate into paragraph four, Section 9, Article I

Amendment XVII:    Incorporate paragraphs one and two of Section 3, Article I

Amendment XVIII:  Delete--Repealed by Amendment XXI

Amendment XIX:    Add with incorporation of Amendment XV above

Amendment XX:     Section 1: Clause 1 to middle of Section 1, Article II
                         Clause 2 to Section 4, Article I
                 Section 2:  Replaces paragraph two, Section 4, Article I
                 Section 3:  Replaces part of Amendment XII
                 Section 4:  Move to Section 2, Amendment XXV and
                         then to paragraph 6, Section 1, Article II

Amendment XXI:  Delete--Used to repeal Amendment XVIII

Amendment XXII:  Section 1: Add after paragraph 5, Section 1, Article II
                 Section 2: Incorporate at end of Article V

Amendment XXIII:  Add to end of Amendment XII; then to Section 1, Article II

Amendment XXIV:  Included with Amendments XV and XIX

Amendment XXV:  Replaces part of Section 1, Article II

Amendment XXVI:  Goes to Section 2, Amendment XIV and ultimately to
                 Section 2 of Article I

Amendment XXVII:  Add after sentence one, Section 6, Article I

Note: Some of these changes are fairly arbitrary since several topics within the Constitution are not well organized. The author has attempted to place them in the most logical place.

# CHAPTER 2  PART 1: BASIC DOCUMENT ANNOTATIONS

CONSTITUTION OF THE UNITED STATES

ANNOTATIONS

We the People of the United States, in Order to form a more perfect Union, establish Justice, insure domestic Tranquility and secure the Blessings of Liberty to ourselves and our provide for the common defence, promote the general Welfare, Posterity, do ordain and establish this Constitution for the United States of America.

Sp (Spelling)

<<<Insert Bill of Rights here

## Article. I.

Section. 1. All legislative Powers herein granted shall be vested in a Congress of the United States, which shall consist of a Senate and House of Representatives.

Section. 2. The House of Representatives shall be composed of Members chosen every second Year by the People of the several States, and the Electors in each State shall have the Qualifications requisite for Electors of the most numerous Branch of the State Legislature. No Person shall be a Representative who shall not have attained to the Age of twenty five Years, and been seven Years a Citizen of the United States, and who shall not, when elected, be an Inhabitant of that State in which he shall be chosen.

[Representatives and direct Taxes shall be apportioned among the several States which may be included within this Union, according to their respective Numbers, which shall be determined by adding to the whole Number of free Persons, including those bound to Service for a Term of Years, and excluding Indians not taxed, three fifths of all other Persons.]

Changed by Sec. 2
Amendment XIV

The actual Enumeration shall be made within three Years after the first Meeting of the Congress of the United States, and within every subsequent Term often Years, in such Manner as they shall by Law direct. The number of Representatives shall not exceed one for every thirty Thousand, but each State shall have at Least one Representative; *and until such enumeration shall be made, the State of New Hampshire shall be entitled to chuse three, Massachusetts eight, Rhode-Island and Providence Plantations one, Connecticut five, New-York six, New Jersey four, Pennsylvania eight, Delaware one, Maryland six, Virginia ten, North Carolina five, South Carolina five, and Georgia three.*

Delete after semicolon
**UPOOE**
(**U**nnecessary, **P**art **O**f **O**riginal **E**stablishment)

When vacancies happen in the Representation from any State, the Executive Authority thereof shall issue Writs of Election to fill such Vacancies. The House of Representatives shall chuse their Speaker and other Officers; and shall have the sole Power of Impeachment.

Sp

Section. 3. [The Senate of the United States shall be composed of two Senators from each State, chosen by the Legislature thereof, for six Years; and each Senator shall have one Vote.] *Immediately after they shall be assembled in Consequence of the first Election,* they shall be divided as equally as may be into three Classes. *The Seats of the Senators of the first Class shall be vacated at the    Expiration of the second Year, of the second Class at the Expiration of the fourth Year, and of the third Class at the Expiration of the sixth Year*, so that one third may be chosen every second Year; [and if Vacancies happen by Resignation, or otherwise, during the Recess of the Legislature of any State, the Executive thereof may make temporary Appointments until the next Meeting of the Legislature, which shall then fill such Vacancies.] No Person shall be a Senator who shall not have attained to the Age of thirty Years, and been nine Years a Citizen of the United States, and who shall not, when elected, be an Inhabitant of that State for which he shall be chosen.

Changed by
Amend. XVII

UPOOE

Changed by
Amend. XVII

The Vice President of the United States shall be President of the Senate, but shall have no Vote, unless they be equally divided.

The Senate shall chuse their other Officers, and also a President pro tempore, in the Absence of the Vice President, or when he shall exercise the Office of President of the United States.

Sp

The Senate shall have the sole Power to try all Impeachments. When sitting for that Purpose, they shall be on Oath or Affirmation. When the President of the United States is tried, the Chief Justice shall preside: And no Person shall be convicted without the Concurrence of two thirds of the Members present.

Judgment in Cases of Impeachment shall not extend further than to removal from Office, and disqualification to hold and enjoy any Office of honor, Trust or Profit under the United States: but the Party convicted shall nevertheless be liable and subject to Indictment, Trial, Judgment and Punishment, according to Law.

Section. 4. The Times, Places and Manner of holding Elections for Senators and Representatives, shall be prescribed in each State by the Legislature thereof; but the Congress may at any time by Law make or alter such Regulations, except as to the Places of chusing Senators.

Sp

<<<Insert Clause 2, Sec. 1, Amend. XX

Changed by Sec. 2 Amend. XX

The Congress shall assemble at least once in every Year, and such Meeting shall be [on the first Monday in December.] unless they shall by Law appoint a different Day.

Section. 5. Each House shall be the Judge of the Elections, Returns and Qualifications of its own Members, and a Majority of each shall constitute a Quorum to do Business; but a smaller Number may adjourn from day to day, and may be authorized to compel the Attendance of absent Members, in such Manner, and under such Penalties as each House may provide.

Each House may determine the Rules of its Proceedings, punish its Members for disorderly Behaviour, and, with the Concurrence of two thirds, expel a Member.

Sp

Each House shall keep a Journal of its Proceedings, and from time to time publish the same, excepting such Parts as may in their Judgment require Secrecy; and the Yeas and Nays of the Members of either House on any question shall, at the Desire of one fifth of those Present, be entered on the Journal.

Neither House, during the Session of Congress, shall, without the Consent of the other, adjourn for more than three days, nor to any other Place than that in which the two Houses shall be sitting.

Section. 6. The Senators and Representatives shall receive a Compensation for their Services, to be ascertained by Law, and paid out of the Treasury of the United States.

<<<Add Amend. XXVII

They shall in all Cases, except Treason, Felony and Breach of the Peace, be privileged from Arrest during their Attendance at the Session of their respective Houses, and in going to and returning from the same; and for any Speech or Debate in either House, they shall not be questioned in any other Place.

No Senator or Representative shall, during the Time for which he was elected, be appointed to any civil Office under the Authority of the United States, which shall have been created, or the Emoluments whereof shall have been encreased during such time; and no Person holding any Office under the United States, shall be a Member of either House during his Continuance in Office.

Sp

Section. 7. All Bills for raising Revenue shall originate in the House of Representatives; but the Senate may propose or concur with Amendments as on other Bills. Every Bill which shall have passed the House of Representatives and the Senate, shall, before it becomes a Law, be presented to the President of the United States; If he approve he shall sign it, but if not he shall return it, with his Objections to that House in which it shall have originated, who shall enter the Objections at large on their Journal, and proceed to reconsider it. If after such Reconsideration two thirds of that House shall agree to pass the Bill, it shall be sent, together with the Objections, to the other House, by which it shall likewise be reconsidered, and if approved by two thirds of that House, it shall become a Law. But in all such Cases the Votes of both Houses shall be determined by yeas and Nays, and the Names of the Persons voting for and against the Bill shall be entered on the Journal of each House respectively. If any Bill shall not be returned by the President within ten Days (Sundays excepted) after it shall have been presented to him, the Same shall be a Law, in like Manner as if he had signed it, unless the Congress by their Adjournment prevent its Return, in which Case it shall not be a Law. Every Order, Resolution, or Vote to which the Concurrence of the Senate and House of Representatives may be necessary (except on a question of Adjournment) shall be presented to the President of the United States; and before the Same shall take Effect, shall be approved by him, or being disapproved by him, shall be repassed by two thirds of the Senate and House of Representatives, according to the Rules and Limitations prescribed in the Case of a Bill.

Sp

Section. 8. The Congress shall have Power To lay and collect Taxes, Duties, Imposts and Excises, to pay the Debts and

provide for the common Defence and general Welfare of the
United States; but all Duties, Imposts and Excises shall be
uniform throughout the United States;

To borrow Money on the credit of the United States;

To regulate Commerce with foreign Nations, and among
the several States, and with the Indian Tribes;

To establish an uniform Rule of Naturalization, and
uniform Laws on the subject of Bankruptcies throughout the
United States;

To coin Money, regulate the Value thereof', and of foreign
Coin, and fix the Standard of Weights and Measures;

To provide for the Punishment of counterfeiting the
Securities and current Coin of the United States;

To establish Post Offices and post Roads;

To promote the Progress of Science and useful Arts, by
securing for limited Times to Authors and Inventors the
exclusive Right to their respective Writings and Discoveries;

To constitute Tribunals inferior to the supreme Court;

To define and punish Piracies and Felonies committed on
the high Seas, and Offenses against the Law of Nations;

To declare War, grant Letters of Marque and Reprisal, and
make Rules concerning Captures on Land and Water;

To raise and support Armies, but no Appropriation of
Money to that Use shall be for a longer Term than two Years;
To provide and maintain a Navy;

To make Rules for the Government and Regulation of the
land and naval Forces;

To provide for calling forth the Militia to execute the Laws
of the Union, suppress Insurrections and repel Invasions;

To provide for organizing, arming, and disciplining, the
Militia, and for governing such Part of them as may be
employed in the Service of the United States, reserving to the
States respectively, the Appointment of the Officers, and the
Authority of training the Militia according to the discipline
prescribed by Congress;

To exercise exclusive Legislation in all Cases whatsoever,
over such District (not exceeding ten Miles square) as may, by
Cession of particular States, and the Acceptance of Congress,
become the Seat of the Government of the United States, and to
exercise like Authority over all Places purchased by the
Consent of the Legislature of the State in which the Same shall
be, for the Erection of Forts, Magazines, Arsenals, dock-Yards
and other needful Buildings;--And

To make all Laws which shall be necessary and proper for
carrying into Execution the foregoing Powers, and all other
Powers vested by this Constitution in the Government of the

United States or in any Department or Officer thereof.

Section. 9. *The Migration or Importation of such Persons as any of the States now existing shall think proper to admit, shall not be prohibited by the Congress prior to the Year one thousand eight hundred and eight, but a Tax or duly may be imposed on such Importation, not exceeding ten dollars for each Person.*

UPOOE

The Privilege of the Writ of Habeas Corpus shall not be suspended, unless when in Cases of Rebellion or Invasion the public Safety may require it.

No Bill of Attainder or ex post facto Law shall be passed.

No Capitation, or other direct, Tax shall be laid, [unless in Proportion to the Census or Enumeration herein before directed to be taken.]

Changed by Amend. XVI

No Tax or Duty shall be laid on Articles exported from any State.

No Preference shall be given by any Regulation of Commerce or Revenue to the Ports of one State over those of another: nor shall Vessels bound to, or from, one State, be obliged to enter, clear, or pay Duties in another.

No Money shall be drawn from the Treasury, but in Consequence of Appropriations made by Law; and a regular Statement and Account of the Receipts and Expenditures of all public Money shall be published from time to time.

No Title of Nobility shall be granted by the United States: And no Person holding any Office of Profit or Trust under them, shall, without the Consent of the Congress, accept of any present, Emolument, Office, or Title, of any kind whatever, from any King, Prince, or foreign State.

Section. 10. No State shall enter into any Treaty, Alliance, or Confederation; grant Letters of Marque and Reprisal; coin Money; emit Bills of Credit; make any Thing but gold and silver Coin a Tender in Payment of Debts; pass any Bill of Attainder, ex post facto Law, or Law impairing the Obligation of Contracts, or grant any Title of Nobility.

No State shall, without the Consent of the Congress, lay any Imposts or Duties on Imports or Exports, except what may be absolutely necessary for executing it's inspection Laws: and the net Produce of all Duties and Imposts, laid by any State on Imports or Exports, shall be for the Use of the Treasury of the United States; and all such Laws shall be subject to the Revision and Control of the Congress.

No State shall, without the Consent of Congress, lay any Duty of Tonnage, keep Troops, or Ships of War in time of Peace, enter into any Agreement or Compact with another State, or with a foreign Power, or engage in War, unless actually invaded, or in such imminent Danger as will not admit of delay.


## Article. II.

Section. 1. The executive Power shall be vested in a President of the United States of America. He shall hold his Office during the Term of four Years, and, together with the Vice President, chosen for the same Term, be elected, as follows:

Each State shall appoint, in such Manner as the Legislature thereof may direct, a Number of Electors, equal to the whole Number of Senators and Representatives to which the State may be entitled in the Congress: but no Senator or Representative, or Person holding an Office of Trust or Profit under the United States, shall be appointed an Elector.

[The Electors shall meet in their respective States, and vote by Ballot for two Persons, of whom one at least shall not be an Inhabitant of the same State with themselves. And they shall make a List of all the Persons voted for, and of the Number of Votes for each: which List they shall sign and certify, and transmit sealed to the Seat of the Government of the United States, directed to the President of the Senate. The President of the Senate shall, in the Presence of the Senate and House of Representatives, open all the Certificates, and the Votes shall then be counted. The Person having the greatest Number of Votes shall be the President, if such Number be a Majority of the whole Number of Electors appointed; and if there be more than one who have such Majority, and have an equal Number of Votes, then the House of Representatives shall immediately chuse by Ballot one of them for President: and if no Person have a Majority, then from the five highest on the List the said House shall in like Manner chuse the President. But in chusing the President, the Votes shall be taken by States, the Representation from each State having one Vote: A quorum for this Purpose shall consist of a Member or Members from two thirds of the States, and a Majority of all the States shall be

| Changed by Amend. XII |

necessary to a Choice. In every Case, after the Choice of the President, the Person having the greatest Number of Votes of the Electors shall be the Vice President. But if there should remain two or more who have equal Votes, the Senate shall chuse from them by Ballot the Vice President.]

The Congress may determine the Time of chusing the Electors, and the Day on which they shall give their Votes; which Day shall be the same throughout the United States.

| Sp |
|---|

No Person except a natural born Citizen, or a Citizen of the United States, at the time of the Adoption of this Constitution, shall be eligible to the Office of President; neither shall any person be eligible to that Office who shall not have attained to the Age of thirty five Years, and been fourteen Years a Resident within the United States.

<<<Add Sec.1, Amend. XXII

<<<Add Clause 1, Sec.1, Amend. XX

[In Case of the Removal of the President from Office, or of his Death, Resignation, or Inability to discharge the Powers and Duties of the said Office, the Same shall devolve on the Vice President, and the Congress may by Law provide for the Case of Removal, Death, Resignation or Inability, both of the President and Vice President, declaring what Officer shall then act as President, and such Officer shall act accordingly, until the Disability be removed, or a President shall be elected.]

Changed by Amend. XXV

The President shall, at stated Times, receive for his Services, a Compensation, which shall neither be increased nor diminished during the Period for which he shall have been elected, and he shall not receive within that Period any other Emolument from the United States, or any of them.

Before he enter on the Execution of his Office, he shall take the following Oath or Affirmation:--"I do solemnly swear (or affirm) that I will faithfully execute the Office of President of the United States, and will to the best of my Ability, preserve, protect and defend the Constitution of the United States."

Section. 2. The President shall be Commander in Chief of the Army and Navy of the United States, and of the Militia of the several States, when called into the actual Service of the United States; he may require the Opinion, in writing, of the principal Officer in each of the executive Departments, upon any Subject relating to the Duties of their respective Offices, and he shall have Power to grant Reprieves and Pardons for Offenses against the United States, except in Cases of Impeachment.

He shall have Power, by and with the Advice and Consent of the Senate, to make Treaties, provided two thirds of the Senators present concur; and he shall nominate, and by and with the Advice and Consent of the Senate, shall appoint Ambassadors, other public Ministers and Consuls, Judges of the supreme Court, and all other Officers of the United States, whose Appointments are not herein otherwise provided for, and which shall be established by Law: but the Congress may by Law vest the Appointment of such inferior Officers, as they think proper, in the President alone, in the Courts of Law, or in the Heads of Departments.

The President shall have Power to fill up all Vacancies that may happen during the Recess of the Senate, by granting Commissions which shall expire at the End of their next Session.

Section. 3. He shall from time to time give to the Congress Information of the State of the Union, and recommend to their Consideration such Measures as he shall judge necessary and expedient; he may, on extraordinary Occasions, convene both Houses, or either of them, and in Case of Disagreement between them, with Respect to the Time of Adjournment, he may adjourn them to such Time as he shall think proper; he shall receive Ambassadors and other public Ministers; he shall take Care that the Laws be faithfully executed, and shall Commission all the Officers of the United States.

Section. 4. The President, Vice President and all civil Officers of the United States, shall be removed from Office on Impeachment for, and Conviction of, Treason, Bribery, or other high Crimes and Misdemeanors.


# Article. III.
Section. 1. The judicial Power of the United States, shall be vested in one supreme Court, and in such inferior Courts as the Congress may from time to time ordain and establish. The Judges, both of the supreme and inferior Courts, shall hold

their Offices during good Behaviour, and shall, at stated Times, receive for their Services, a Compensation, which shall not be diminished during their Continuance in Office.

Sp

Section. 2. The judicial Power shall extend to all Cases, in Law and Equity, arising under this Constitution, the Laws of the United States, and Treaties made, or which shall be made, under their Authority;--to all Cases affecting Ambassadors, other public Ministers and Consuls;-- to all Cases of admiralty and maritime Jurisdiction;--to Controversies to which the United States shall be a Party;--to Controversies between two or more States;--[between a State and Citizens of another State;--] between Citizens of different States,-- between Citizens of the same State claiming Lands under Grants of different States, [and between a State, or the Citizens thereof, and foreign States, Citizens or Subjects.]

Changed by Amend. XI

Changed by Amend. XI

In all Cases affecting Ambassadors, other public Ministers and Consuls, and those in which a State shall be Party, the supreme Court shall have original Jurisdiction. In all the other Cases before mentioned, the supreme Court shall have appellate Jurisdiction, both as to Law and Fact, with such Exceptions, and under such Regulations as the Congress shall make.

The Trial of all Crimes, except in Cases of Impeachment; shall be by Jury; and such Trial shall be held in the State where the said Crimes shall have been committed; but when not committed within any State, the Trial shall be at such Place or Places as the Congress may by Law have directed.

Section. 3. Treason against the United States, shall consist only in levying War against them, or in adhering to their Enemies, giving them Aid and Comfort. No Person shall be convicted of Treason unless on the Testimony of two Witnesses to the same overt Act, or on Confession in open Court.

The Congress shall have Power to declare the Punishment of Treason, but no Attainder of Treason shall work Corruption of Blood, or Forfeiture except during the Life of the Person attainted.

<<< Insert Sec. 3, Amend. XIV

## Article. IV.

Section. 1. Full Faith and Credit shall be given in each State to the public Acts, Records, and judicial Proceedings of every other State; And the Congress may by general Laws prescribe the Manner in which such Acts, Records and Proceedings shall be proved, and the Effect thereof.

Section. 2. The Citizens of each State shall be entitled to all Privileges and Immunities of Citizens in the several States.

> <<< Add Amend. XV

A Person charged in any State with Treason, Felony, or other Crime, who shall flee from Justice, and be found in another State, shall on Demand of the executive Authority of the State from which he fled, be delivered up, to be removed to the State having Jurisdiction of the Crime.

[No Person held to Service or Labour in one State, under the Laws thereof, escaping into another, shall, in Consequence of any Law or Regulation therein, be discharged from such Service or Labour, but shall be delivered up on Claim of the Party to whom such Service or Labour may be due.]

> Changed by Amend. XIII

> <<< Include Sec.1, Amendment XIV

Section. 3. New States may be admitted by the Congress into this Union; but no new State shall be formed or erected within the Jurisdiction of any other State; nor any State be formed by the Junction of two or more States, or Parts of States, without the Consent of the Legislatures of the States concerned as well as of the Congress.

The Congress shall have Power to dispose of and make all needful Rules and Regulations respecting the Territory or other Property belonging to the United States; and nothing in this Constitution shall be so construed as to Prejudice any Claims of the United States, or of any particular State.

Section. 4. The United States shall guarantee to every State in this Union a Republican Form of Government, and shall protect each of them against Invasion; and on Application of the Legislature, or of the Executive (when the Legislature cannot be convened) against domestic Violence.

## Article. V.

The Congress, whenever two thirds of both Houses shall deem it necessary, shall propose Amendments to this Constitution, or, on the Application of the Legislatures of two thirds of the several States, shall call a Convention for proposing Amendments, which, in either Case, shall be valid to all Intents and Purposes, as Part of this Constitution, when ratified by the Legislatures of three fourths of the several States, or by Conventions in three fourths thereof, as the one or the other Mode of Ratification may be proposed by the Congress;

*Provided that no Amendment which may be made prior to the Year One thousand eight hundred and eight shall in any Manner affect the first and fourth Clauses in the Ninth Section of the first Article;* and that no State, without its Consent, shall be deprived of it's equal Suffrage in the Senate.

UPOOE

<<< Incorporate Sec. 2, Amend. XIII and XXII

## Article. VI

All Debts contracted and Engagements entered into, before the Adoption of this Constitution, shall be as valid against the United States under this Constitution, *as under the Confederation*
.

UPOOE

<<< Add Sec. 4, Amend. XIV

This Constitution, and the Laws of the United States which shall be made in Pursuance thereof; and all Treaties made, or which shall be made, under the Authority of the United States, shall be the supreme Law of the Land; and the Judges in every State shall be bound thereby, any Thing in the Constitution or Laws of any State to the Contrary notwithstanding.

The Senators and Representatives before mentioned, and the Members of the several State Legislatures, and all executive and judicial Officers, both of the United States and of the several States, shall be bound by Oath or Affirmation, to support this Constitution; but no religious Test shall ever be required as a Qualification to any Office or public Trust under the United States.

## Article. VII.

The Ratification of the Conventions of *nine* States, shall be sufficient for the Establishment of this Constitution between the States so ratifying the Same.

UPOOE

Done in Convention by *the Unanimous Consent of the States present the Seventeenth Day of September in the Year of our Lord one thousand seven hundred and Eighty seven and of the Independence of the United States of America the Twelfth In Witness whereof We have hereunto subscribed our Names.*

UPOOE

Note:  This concludes annotation of the basic document

# CHAPT. 2, PART 2: ANNOTATIONS of PRESENT AMENDMENTS

Amendment I. Congress shall make no law respecting an establishment of religion, or prohibiting the free exercise thereof; or abridging the freedom of speech, or of the press, or the right of the people peaceably to assemble, and to petition the Government for a redress of grievances.

Amendment II. A well regulated Militia, being necessary to the security of a free State, the right of the people to keep and bear Arms, shall not be infringed.

Amendment III. No Soldier shall, in time of peace be quartered in any house, without the consent of the Owner, nor in time of war, but in a manner to be prescribed by law.

> ANNOTATIONS
>
> Complete Bill of Rights moved to just after Preamble

Amendment IV. The right of the people to be secure in their persons, houses, papers, and effects, against unreasonable searches and seizures, shall not be violated, and no Warrants shall issue, but upon probable cause, supported by Oath or affirmation, and particularly describing the place to be searched, and the persons or things to be seized.

Amendment V. No person shall be held to answer for a capital, or otherwise infamous crime, unless on a presentment or indictment of a Grand Jury, except in cases arising in the land or naval forces, or in the Militia, when in actual service in time of War or public danger; nor shall any person be subject for the same offence to be twice put in jeopardy of life or limb, nor shall be compelled in any criminal case to be a witness against himself, nor be deprived of life, liberty, or property, without due process of law; nor shall private property be taken for public use without just compensation.

Amendment VI. In all criminal prosecutions, the accused shall enjoy the right to a speedy and public trial, by an impartial jury of the State and district wherein the crime shall have been committed; which district shall have been previously ascertained by law, and to be informed of the nature and cause of the accusation; to be confronted with the witnesses against him; to have compulsory process for obtaining witnesses in his favor, and to have the assistance of counsel for his defence.

defense

Amendment VII. In Suits at common law, where the value in controversy shall exceed twenty dollars, the right of trial by jury shall be preserved, and no fact tried by a jury shall be otherwise re-examined in any Court of the United States, than according to the rules of the common law.

Amendment VIII. Excessive bail shall not be required, nor excessive fines imposed, nor cruel and unusual punishments inflicted.

Amendment IX. The enumeration in the Constitution of certain rights shall not be construed to deny or disparage others retained by the people.

Amendment X. The powers not delegated to the United States by the Constitution, nor prohibited by it to the States, are reserved to the States respectively, or to the people.

Amendment XI. The Judicial power of the United States shall not be construed to extend to any suit in law or equity, commenced or prosecuted against one of the United States by Citizens of another State, or by Citizens or Subjects of any Foreign State.

To Sec. 2, Art. III

Amendment XII. The Electors shall meet in their respective states, and vote by ballot for President and Vice President, one of whom, at least, shall not be an inhabitant of the same state with themselves; they shall name in their ballots the person voted for as President, and in distinct ballots the person voted for as Vice-President, and they shall make distinct lists of all persons voted for as President, and of all persons voted for as Vice-President, and of the number of votes for each, which lists they shall sign and certify, and transmit sealed to the seat of the government of the United States, directed to the President of the Senate;--The President of the Senate shall, in the presence of the Senate and House of Representatives, open all the certificates and the votes shall then be counted;--The person having the greatest number of votes for President, shall be the President, if such number be a majority of the whole number of Electors appointed; and if no person have such majority, then from the persons having the highest numbers not exceeding three on the list of those voted for as President, the House of Representatives shall choose immediately, by ballot, the President. But in choosing the President, the votes shall be taken by states, the representation from each state having one vote; a quorum for this purpose shall consist of a member or members from two-thirds of the states, and a majority of all the states shall be necessary to a choice.

To Sec. 1, Art. II

[And if the House of Representatives shall not choose a President whenever the right of choice shall devolve upon them, before the fourth day of March next following, then the Vice President shall act as President, as in the case of the death or other constitutional disability of the President---]

Amended Amendment Changed by Sec. 3, Amend. XX

The person having the greatest number of votes as Vice-President, shall be the Vice-President, if such number be a majority of the whole number of Electors appointed, and if no person have a majority, then from the two highest numbers on the list, the Senate shall choose the Vice-President; a quorum for the purpose shall consist of two-thirds of the whole number of Senators, and a majority of the whole number shall be necessary to a choice. But no person constitutionally ineligible to the office of President shall be eligible to that of Vice-President of the United States.

<< Insert Amendment XXIII

Amendment XIII.

 Section 1. Neither slavery nor involuntary servitude, except as a punishment for crime whereof the party shall have been duly convicted, shall exist within the United States, or any place subject to their jurisdiction.

To Sec. 2, Art. IV

 Section 2. Congress shall have power to enforce this article by appropriate legislation.

**Unnecessary, Just Needed Once** (UJNO) Put in Art. V

Amendment XIV.
 Section 1. All persons born or naturalized in the United States and subject to the jurisdiction thereof, are citizens of the United States and of the State wherein they reside. No State shall make or enforce any law which shall abridge the privileges or immunities of citizens of the United States; nor shall any State deprive any person of life, liberty, or property, without due process of law; nor deny to any person within its jurisdiction the equal protection of the laws.

To Sec. 2, Art. IV

Section 2. Representatives shall be apportioned among the several States according to their respective numbers, counting the whole number of persons in each State, excluding Indians not taxed. But when the right to vote at any election for the choice of electors for President and Vice President of the United States, Representatives in Congress, the Executive and Judicial officers of a State, or the members of the Legislature thereof, is denied to any of the male inhabitants of such State, [ being twenty-one years of age,] and citizens of the United States, or in any way abridged, except for participation in rebellion, or other crime, the basis of representation therein shall be reduced in the proportion which the number of such male citizens shall bear to the whole number of male citizens twenty-one years of age in such State.

Changes part of Sec. 2, Art. I

Amended Amendment Changed by Sec. 1, Amend. XXVI

 Section 3. No person shall be a Senator or Representative in Congress, or elector of President and Vice President, or hold any office, civil or military, under the United States, or under any State, who, having previously taken an oath, as a member of Congress, or as an officer of the United States, or as a member of any State legislature, or as an executive or judicial officer of any State, to support the Constitution of the United States, shall have engaged in insurrection or rebellion against

To Sec. 3, Art. III

the same, or given aid or comfort to the enemies thereof. But Congress may by a vote of two-thirds of each House, remove such disability.

Section 4. The validity of the public debt of the United States, authorized by law, including debts incurred for payment of pensions and bounties for services in suppressing insurrection or rebellion, shall not be questioned. But neither the United States nor any State shall assume or pay any debt or obligation incurred in aid of insurrection or rebellion against the United States, *or any claim for the loss or emancipation of any slave;* but all such debts, obligations and claims shall be held illegal and void.

*Section 5. The Congress shall have power to enforce, by appropriate legislation, the provisions of this article.*

Amendment XV. Section 1. The right of citizens of the United States to vote shall not be denied or abridged by the United States or by any State on account of race, color, *or previous condition of servitude.*

*Section 2. The Congress shall have power to enforce this article by appropriate legislation.*

Amendment XVI. The Congress shall have power to lay and collect taxes on incomes, from whatever source derived, without apportionment among the several States, and without regard to any census or enumeration.

Amendment XVII. The Senate of the United States shall be composed of two Senators from each State, elected by the people thereof, for six years; and each Senator shall have one vote. The electors in each State shall have the qualifications requisite for electors of the most numerous branch of the State legislatures.

When vacancies happen in the representation of any State in the Senate, the executive authority of such State shall issue writs of election to fill such vacancies: Provided, That the legislature of any State may empower the executive thereof to make temporary appointments until the people fill the vacancies by election as the legislature may direct.

*This amendment shall not be so construed as to affect the election or term of any Senator chosen before it becomes valid as part of the Constitution.*

Amendment XVIII.
[Section 1. After one year from the ratification of this article the manufacture, sale, or transportation of intoxicating liquors within, the importation thereof into, or the exportation thereof from the United

---

**Margin notes:**

Add after sentence one Art. VI

**Unnecessary After Emancipation (UAE)**

UJNO

Add after sentence one, Sec. 2, Art. IV UAE

UJNO

Incorporate paragraph 4, Sec. 9, Art. I

To Sec. 3, Art. I

To Sec. 3, Art. I

**Unnecessary After Approval (UAA)**

Repealed by Amendment XXI

States and all territory subject to the jurisdiction thereof for beverage purposes is hereby prohibited.

Section 2. The Congress and the several States shall have concurrent power to enforce this article by appropriate legislation.

Section 3. This article shall be inoperative unless it shall have been ratified as an amendment to the Constitution by the legislatures of the several States, as provided in the Constitution, within seven years from the date of the submission hereof to the States by the Congress.]

Amendment XIX. The right of citizens of the United States to vote shall not be denied or abridged by the United States or by any State on account of sex.

*Congress shall have power to enforce this article by appropriate legislation.*

Amendment XX. Section 1. The terms of the President and Vice President shall end at noon on the 20th day of January, and the terms of Senators and Representatives at noon on the 3d day of January, of the years in which such terms would have ended *if this article had not been ratified; and the terms of their successors shall then begin.*

Section 2. The Congress shall assemble at least once in every year, and such meeting shall begin at noon on the 3d day of January, unless they shall by law appoint a different day.

Section 3. If, at the time fixed for the beginning of the term of the President, the President elect shall have died, the Vice President elect shall become President. If a President shall not have been chosen before the time fixed for the beginning of his term, or if the President elect shall have failed to qualify, then the Vice President elect shall act as President until a President shall have qualified; and the Congress may by law provide for the case wherein neither a President elect nor a Vice President elect shall have qualified, declaring who shall then act as President, or the manner in which one who is to act shall be selected, and such person shall act accordingly until a President or Vice President shall have qualified.

Section 4. The Congress may by law provide for the case of the death of any of the persons from whom the House of Representatives may choose a President whenever the right of choice shall have devolved upon them, and for the case of the death of any of the persons from whom the Senate may choose a Vice President whenever the right of choice shall have devolved upon them.

---

Repealed by Amendment XXI

Include with incorporation of Amendment XV

UJNO

Clause 1 to Sec. 1, Art. II
Clause 2 to Sec. 4, Art. I
UAA

Replaces paragraph 2, Sec. 4, Art. I

Replaces part of Amendment XII

Move to Sec. 2, Amend. XXV, then to paragraph 6, Sec. 1, Art. II

*Section 5. Sections 1 and 2 shall take effect on the 15th day of October following the ratification of this article.*

| | UAA |

*Section 6. This article shall be inoperative unless it shall have been ratified as an amendment to the Constitution by the legislatures of three-fourths of the several States within seven years from the date of its submission.*

| | UAA |

*Amendment XXI. Section 1. The eighteenth article of amendment to the Constitution of the United States is hereby repealed.*
*Section 2. The transportation or importation into any State, Territory, or possession of the United States for delivery or use therein of intoxicating liquors, in violation of the laws thereof, is hereby prohibited. Section 3. This article shall be inoperative unless it shall have been ratified as an amendment to the Constitution by conventions in the several States, as provided in the Constitution, within seven years from the date of the submission hereof to the States by the Congress.*

| | Delete, used to repeal Amend. XVIII |

Amendment XXII. Section 1. No person shall be elected to the office of the President more than twice, and no person who has held the office of President, or acted as President, for more than two years of a term to which some other person was elected President shall be elected to the office of the President more than once.

| | Add to paragh. 5, Sec. 1, Art. II |

*But this Article shall not apply to any person holding the office of President when this Article was proposed by the Congress, and shall not prevent any person who may be holding the office of President, or acting as President, during the term within which this Article becomes operative from holding the office of President or acting as President during the remainder of such term.*

| | UAA |

Section 2. This article shall be inoperative unless it shall have been ratified as an amendment to the Constitution by the legislatures of three-fourths of the several States within seven years from the date of its submission to the States by the Congress.

| | General statement, incorporate at end of Art. V |

Amendment XXIII. Section 1. The District constituting the seat of Government of the United States shall appoint in such manner as the Congress may direct: A number of electors of President and Vice President equal to the whole number of Senators and Representatives in Congress to which the District would be entitled if it were a State, but in no event more than the least populous State; they shall be in addition to those appointed by the States, but they shall be considered, for the purposes of the election of President and Vice President, to be electors appointed by a State; and they shall meet in the District and perform such duties as provided by the twelfth article of amendment.

| | Add at end of Amendment XII, then goes to Sec. 1, Art. II |

*Section 2. The Congress shall have power to enforce this article by appropriate legislation.*

| | UJNO |

Amendment XXIV. Section 1. The right of citizens of the United States to vote in any primary or other election for President or Vice President, for electors for President or Vice President, or for Senator or Representative in Congress, shall not be denied or abridged by the United States or any State by reason of failure to pay any poll tax or other tax.

*Section 2. The Congress shall have power to enforce this article by appropriate legislation.*

Amendment XXV. Section 1. In case of the removal of the President from office or of his death or resignation, the Vice President shall become President.

Section 2. Whenever there is a vacancy in the office of the Vice President, the President shall nominate a Vice President who shall take office upon confirmation by a majority vote of both Houses of Congress.

Section 3. Whenever the President transmits to the President pro tempore of the Senate and the Speaker of the House of Representatives his written declaration that he is unable to discharge the powers and duties of his office, and until he transmits to them a written declaration to the contrary, such powers and duties shall be discharged by the Vice President as Acting President.

Section 4. Whenever the Vice President and a majority of either the principal officers of the executive departments or of such other body as Congress may by law provide, transmit to the President pro tempore of the Senate and the Speaker of the House of Representatives their written declaration that the President is unable to discharge the powers and duties of his office, the Vice President shall immediately assume the powers and duties of the office as Acting President. Thereafter, when the President transmits to the President pro tempore of the Senate and the Speaker of the House of Representatives his written declaration that no inability exists, he shall resume the powers and duties of his office unless the Vice President and a majority of either the principal officers of the executive department or of such other body as Congress may by law provide, transmit within four days to the President pro tempore of the Senate and the Speaker of the House of Representatives their written declaration that the President is unable to discharge the powers and duties of his office. Thereupon Congress shall decide the issue, assembling within forty-eight hours for that purpose if not in session. If the Congress, within twenty-one days after receipt of the latter written declaration, or, if Congress is not in session, within twenty-one days after Congress is required to assemble, determines by two-thirds vote of both Houses that the President is unable to discharge the powers and duties of his office, the Vice President shall

Include with Amend. XV and XIX which go to Sec. 2, Art. IV

UJNO

This Amendment replaces part of Sec. 1, Art II

continue to discharge the same as Acting President; otherwise, the President shall resume the powers and duties of his office.

Amendment XXVI. Section 1. The right of citizens of the United States, who are eighteen years of age or older, to vote shall not be denied or abridged by the United States or by any State on account of age.

*Section 2. The Congress shall have power to enforce this article by appropriate legislation.*

Amendment XXVII. No law, varying the compensation for the services of the Senators and Representatives, shall take effect, until an election of Representatives shall have intervened.

To Sec. 2, Amend. XIV, then to Sec. 2, Art.IV

UJNO

Add after sentence one, Sec. 6, Art. I

Note: This concludes the annotation of the current Amendments (2010).

## CHAPTER 2: PART 3
## INCORPORATION OF ANNOTATED CHANGES

CONSTITUTION OF THE UNITED STATES

PREAMBLE:

We the People of the United States, in Order to form a more perfect

Union, establish Justice, insure domestic Tranquility, provide for the

common defense, promote the general Welfare, and secure the Blessings

of Liberty to ourselves and our Posterity, do ordain and establish this

Constitution for the United States of America.

defense
spelling fix

<< Bill of
Rights
Inserted

## CITIZEN'S BILL OF RIGHTS:

First Right  (Amend. I). Congress shall make no law respecting an
establishment of religion, or prohibiting the free exercise thereof; or abridging
the freedom of speech, or of the press, or the right of the people peaceably to
assemble, and to petition the Government for a redress of grievances.

Second Right  (Amend. II). A well regulated Militia, being necessary to the security of a
free State, the right of the people to keep and bear Arms, shall not be infringed.

Third Right (Amend. III). No Soldier shall, in time of peace be quartered in any house,
without the consent of the Owner, nor in time of war, but in a manner to be prescribed by
law.

Fourth Right (Amend. IV). The right of the people to be secure in their persons, houses,
papers, and effects, against unreasonable searches and seizures, shall not be violated, and
no Warrants shall issue, but upon probable cause, supported by Oath or affirmation, and
particularly describing the place to be searched, and the persons or things to be seized.

Fifth Right (Amend. V). No person shall be held to answer for a capital, or otherwise
infamous crime, unless on a presentment or indictment of a Grand Jury, except in cases
arising in the land or naval forces, or in the Militia, when in actual service in time of War
or public danger; nor shall any person be subject for the same offence to be twice put in
jeopardy of life or limb, nor shall be compelled in any criminal case to be a witness
against himself, nor be deprived of life, liberty, or property, without due process of law;
nor shall private property be taken for public use without just compensation.

Sixth Right (Amend. VI). In all criminal prosecutions, the accused shall
enjoy the right to a speedy and public trial, by an impartial jury of the
State and district wherein the crime shall have been committed; which

district shall have been previously ascertained by law, and to be informed of the nature and cause of the accusation; to be confronted with the witnesses against him; to have compulsory process for obtaining witnesses in his favor, and to have the assistance of counsel for his defense.

defense

Seventh Right (Amend. VII). In Suits at common law, where the value in controversy shall exceed twenty dollars, the right of trial by jury shall be preserved, and no fact tried by a jury shall be otherwise re-examined in any Court of the United States, than according to the rules of the common law.

Eighth Right (Amend. VIII). Excessive bail shall not be required, nor excessive fines imposed, nor cruel and unusual punishments inflicted.

Ninth Right (Amend. IX). The enumeration in the Constitution of certain rights shall not be construed to deny or disparage others retained by the people.

Tenth Right (Amend. X). The powers not delegated to the United States by the Constitution, nor prohibited by it to the States, are reserved to the States respectively, or to the people.

## ARTICLE I: THE CONGRESS

Title added

Section. 1. All legislative Powers herein granted shall be vested in a Congress of the United States, which shall consist of a Senate and House of Representatives.

Section. 2. The House of Representatives shall be composed of Members chosen every second Year by the People of the several States, and the Electors in each State shall have the Qualifications requisite for Electors of the most numerous Branch of the State Legislature. No Person shall be a Representative who shall not have attained to the Age of twenty five Years, and been seven Years a Citizen of the United States, and who shall not, when elected, be an Inhabitant of that State in which he shall be chosen.

Representatives shall be apportioned among the several States according to their respective numbers, counting the whole number of persons in each State, excluding Indians not taxed. But when the right to vote at any election for the choice of electors for President and Vice President of the United States, Representatives in Congress, the Executive and Judicial officers of a State, or the members of the Legislature thereof, is denied to any of the male inhabitants of such State, being twenty-one years of age, and citizens of the United States, or in any way abridged, except for participation in rebellion, or other crime, the basis of representation therein shall be reduced in the proportion which the number of such male citizens shall bear to the whole number of male citizens twenty-one years of age in such State. (Sec. 2, Amend. XIV)

Sentence replaced with Sec. 2 of Amend. XIV

The actual Enumeration shall be made within three Years after the first Meeting of the Congress of the United States, and within every subsequent Term of ten Years, in such Manner as they shall by Law direct. The number of Representatives shall not exceed one for every thirty Thousand, but each State shall have at Least one Representative.

<<Clause removed: "and until----- Georgia three." **U**nnecessary **P**art of **O**riginal **E**stablishment (UPOOE) Sp **choo**se

When vacancies happen in the Representation from any State, the Executive Authority thereof shall issue Writs of Election to fill such Vacancies. The House of Representatives shall choose their Speaker and other Officers; and shall have the sole Power of Impeachment.

Section. 3. The Senate of the United States shall be composed of two Senators from each State, elected by the people thereof, for six years; and each Senator shall have one vote. The electors in each State shall have the qualifications requisite for electors of the most numerous branch of the State legislatures.

Clause replaced by Amend. XVII

Portion removed UPOOE

Senators shall be divided as equally as may be into three Classes, so that one third may be chosen every second Year.

Portions removed UPOOE

Clause replaced by Amend. XVII

When vacancies happen in the representation of any State in the Senate, the executive authority of such State shall issue writs of election to fill such vacancies: Provided, That the legislature of any State may empower the executive thereof to make temporary appointments until the people fill the vacancies by election as the legislature may direct.

No Person shall be a Senator who shall not have attained to the Age of thirty Years, and been nine Years a Citizen of the United States, and who shall not, when elected, be an Inhabitant of that State for which he shall be chosen.

The Vice President of the United States shall be President of the Senate, but shall have no Vote, unless they be equally divided.

The Senate shall choose their other Officers, and also a President pro tempore, in the Absence of the Vice President, or when he shall exercise the Office of President of the United States.

**choo**se

The Senate shall have the sole Power to try all Impeachments. When sitting for that Purpose, they shall be on Oath or Affirmation. When the President of the United States is tried, the Chief Justice shall preside: And no Person shall be convicted without the Concurrence of two thirds of the Members present.

Judgment in Cases of Impeachment shall not extend further than to removal from Office, and disqualification to hold and enjoy any Office of honor, Trust or Profit under the

United States: but the Party convicted shall nevertheless be liable and subject to Indictment, Trial, Judgment and Punishment, according to Law.

Section. 4. The Times, Places and Manner of holding Elections for Senators and Representatives, shall be prescribed in each State by the Legislature thereof; but the Congress may at any time by Law make or alter such Regulations, except as to the Places of choosing Senators.

The terms of the Senators and Representatives shall end at noon on the 3d day of January. (Clause 2, Sec. 1, Amend. XX)

The Congress shall assemble at least once in every year, and such meeting shall begin at noon on the 3d day of January, unless they shall by law appoint a different day. (Sec. 2, Amend. XX)

Section. 5. Each House shall be the Judge of the Elections, Returns and Qualifications of its own Members, and a Majority of each shall constitute a Quorum to do Business; but a smaller Number may adjourn from day to day, and may be authorized to compel the Attendance of absent Members, in such Manner, and under such Penalties as each House may provide.

Each House may determine the Rules of its Proceedings, punish its Members for disorderly Behavior, and, with the Concurrence of two thirds, expel a Member.

choosing

<<Clause 2, Sec. 1 Amend. XX added

<<Revised paragraph from Amend. XX

Behavior

Each House shall keep a Journal of its Proceedings, and from time to time publish the same, excepting such Parts as may in their Judgment require Secrecy; and the Yeas and Nays of the Members of either House on any question shall, at the Desire of one fifth of those Present, be entered on the Journal.

Neither House, during the Session of Congress, shall, without the Consent of the other, adjourn for more than three days, nor to any other Place than that in which the two Houses shall be sitting.

Section. 6. The Senators and Representatives shall receive a Compensation for their Services, to be ascertained by Law, and paid out of the Treasury of the United States.

No law, varying the compensation for the services of the Senators and Representatives, shall take effect, until an election of Representatives shall have intervened. (Amend. XXVII)

<<Amend. XXVII added

They shall in all Cases, except Treason, Felony and Breach of the Peace, be privileged from Arrest during their Attendance at the Session of their respective Houses, and in going to and returning from the same; and for any Speech or Debate in either House, they shall not be questioned in any other Place.

No Senator or Representative shall, during the Time for which he was elected, be appointed to any civil Office under the Authority of the United States, which shall have been created, or the Emoluments whereof shall have been increased during such time; and no Person holding any Office under the United States, shall be a Member of either House during his Continuance in Office.

increased

Section. 7. All Bills for raising Revenue shall originate in the House of Representatives; but the Senate may propose or concur with Amendments as on other Bills. Every Bill which shall have passed the House of Representatives and the Senate, shall, before it becomes a Law, be presented to the President of the United States; If he approve he shall sign it, but if not he shall return it, with his Objections to that House in which it shall have originated, who shall enter the Objections at large on their Journal, and proceed to reconsider it. If after such Reconsideration two thirds of that House shall agree to pass the Bill, it shall be sent, together with the Objections, to the other House, by which it shall likewise be reconsidered, and if approved by two thirds of that House, it shall become a Law. But in all such Cases the Votes of both Houses shall be determined by yeas and Nays, and the Names of the Persons voting for and against the Bill shall be entered on the Journal of each House respectively. If any Bill shall not be returned by the President within ten Days (Sundays excepted) after it shall have been presented to him, the Same shall be a Law, in like Manner as if he had signed it, unless the Congress by their Adjournment prevent its Return, in which Case it shall not be a Law. Every Order, Resolution, or Vote to which the Concurrence of the Senate and House of Representatives may be necessary (except on a question of Adjournment) shall be presented to the President of the United States; and before the Same shall take Effect, shall be approved by him, or being disapproved by him, shall be re-passed by two thirds of the Senate and House of Representatives, according to the Rules and Limitations prescribed in the Case of a Bill.

re-passed

Section. 8. The Congress shall have Power To lay and collect Taxes, Duties, Imposts and Excises, to pay the Debts and provide for the common Defense and general Welfare of the United States; but all

Defense

Duties, Imposts and Excises shall be uniform throughout the United States;

To borrow Money on the credit of the United States;

To regulate Commerce with foreign Nations, and among the several States, and with the Indian Tribes;

To establish an uniform Rule of Naturalization, and uniform Laws on the subject of Bankruptcies throughout the United States;

To coin Money, regulate the Value thereof, and of foreign Coin, and fix the Standard of Weights and Measures;

To provide for the Punishment of counterfeiting the Securities and current Coin of the United States;

To establish Post Offices and post Roads;

To promote the Progress of Science and useful Arts, by securing for limited Times to Authors and Inventors the exclusive Right to their respective Writings and Discoveries;

To constitute Tribunals inferior to the supreme Court;

To define and punish Piracies and Felonies committed on the high Seas, and Offenses against the Law of Nations;

To declare War, grant Letters of Marque and Reprisal, and make Rules concerning Captures on Land and Water;

To raise and support Armies, but no Appropriation of Money to that Use shall be for a longer Term than two Years;

To provide and maintain a Navy;

To make Rules for the Government and Regulation of the land and naval Forces;

To provide for calling forth the Militia to execute the Laws of the Union, suppress Insurrections and repel Invasions;

To provide for organizing, arming, and disciplining, the Militia, and for governing such Part of them as may be employed in the Service of the United States, reserving to the States respectively, the Appointment of the Officers, and the Authority of training the Militia according to the discipline prescribed by Congress;

To exercise exclusive Legislation in all Cases whatsoever, over such District (not exceeding ten Miles square) as may, by Cession of particular States, and the Acceptance of Congress, become the Seat of the Government of the United States, and to exercise like Authority over all Places purchased by the Consent of the Legislature of the State in which the Same shall be, for the Erection of Forts, Magazines, Arsenals, dock-Yards and other needful Buildings; --And

To make all Laws which shall be necessary and proper for carrying into Execution the foregoing Powers, and all other Powers vested by this Constitution in the Government of the United States or in any Department or Officer thereof.

Section. 9. The Privilege of the Writ of Habeas Corpus shall not be suspended, unless when in Cases of Rebellion or Invasion the public Safety may require it.

    No Bill of Attainder or ex post facto Law shall be passed.

> <<Original first sentence deleted (UPOOE, UAE)

The Congress shall have power to lay and collect taxes on incomes, from whatever source derived, without apportionment among the several States, and without regard to any census or enumeration. (Amend. XVI)

> Sentence Changed by Amend. XVI

No Capitation, or other direct, Tax shall be laid, unless in Proportion to the Census or Enumeration herein before directed to be taken.

No Tax or Duty shall be laid on Articles exported from any State.

No Preference shall be given by any Regulation of Commerce or Revenue to the Ports of one State over those of another: nor shall Vessels bound to, or from, one State, be obliged to enter, clear, or pay Duties in another.

No Money shall be drawn from the Treasury, but in Consequence of Appropriations made by Law; and a regular Statement and Account of the Receipts and Expenditures of all public Money shall be published from time to time.

No Title of Nobility shall be granted by the United States: And no Person holding any Office of Profit or Trust under them, shall, without the Consent of the Congress, accept of any present, Emolument, Office, or Title, of any kind whatever, from any King, Prince, or foreign State.

Section. 10. No State shall enter into any Treaty, Alliance, or Confederation; grant Letters of Marque and Reprisal; coin Money; emit Bills of Credit; make any Thing but gold and silver Coin a Tender in Payment of Debts; pass any Bill of Attainder, ex post facto Law, or Law impairing the Obligation of Contracts, or grant any Title of Nobility.

No State shall, without the Consent of the Congress, lay any Imposts or Duties on Imports or Exports, except what may be absolutely necessary for executing it's inspection Laws: and the net Produce of all Duties and Imposts, laid by any State on Imports or Exports, shall be for the Use of the Treasury of the United States; and all such Laws shall be subject to the Revision and Control of the Congress.

No State shall, without the Consent of Congress, lay any Duty of Tonnage, keep Troops, or Ships of War in time of Peace, enter into any Agreement or Compact with another State, or with a foreign Power, or engage in War, unless actually invaded, or in such imminent Danger as will not admit of delay.

# ARTICLE II: THE EXECUTIVE.

> Title added

Section. 1. The executive Power shall be vested in a President of the United States of America. He shall hold his Office during the Term of four Years, and, together with the Vice President, chosen for the same Term, be elected, as follows:

Each State shall appoint, in such Manner as the Legislature thereof may direct, a Number of Electors, equal to the whole Number of Senators and Representatives to which the

State may be entitled in the Congress: but no Senator or Representative, or Person holding an Office of Trust or Profit under the United States, shall be appointed an Elector.

The Electors shall meet in their respective states, and vote by ballot for President and Vice President, one of whom, at least, shall not be an inhabitant of the same state with themselves; they shall name in their ballots the person voted for as President, and in distinct ballots the person voted for as Vice-President, and they shall make distinct lists of all persons voted for as President, and of all persons voted for as Vice-President, and of the number of votes for each, which lists they shall sign and certify, and transmit sealed to the seat of the government of the United States, directed to the President of the Senate;--The President of the Senate shall, in the presence of the Senate and House of Representatives, open all the certificates and the votes shall then be counted;--The person having the greatest number of votes for President, shall be the President, if such number be a majority of the whole number of Electors appointed; and if no person have such majority, then from the persons having the highest numbers not exceeding three on the list of those voted for as President, the House of Representatives shall choose immediately, by ballot, the President. But in choosing the President, the votes shall be taken by states, the representation from each state having one vote; a quorum for this purpose shall consist of a member or members from two-thirds of the states, and a majority of all the states shall be necessary to a choice.

> Large paragraph changed by Amendment XII

If, at the time fixed for the beginning of the term of the President, the President elect shall have died, the Vice President elect shall become President. If a President shall not have been chosen before the time fixed for the beginning of his term, or if the President elect shall have failed to qualify, then the Vice President elect shall act as President until a President shall have qualified; and the Congress may by law provide for the case wherein neither a President elect nor a Vice President elect shall have qualified, declaring who shall then act as President, or the manner in which one who is to act shall be selected, and such person shall act accordingly until a President or Vice President shall have qualified. (Sec. 3, Amend. XX)

> Amended Amendment changed by Sec. 3, Amend. XX

The person having the greatest number of votes as Vice-President, shall be the Vice-President, if such number be a majority of the whole number of Electors appointed, and if no person have a majority, then from the two highest numbers on the list, the Senate shall choose the Vice-President; a quorum for the purpose shall consist of two-thirds of the whole number of Senators, and a majority of the whole number shall be necessary to a choice. But no person constitutionally ineligible to the office of President shall be eligible to that of Vice-President of the United States. (Amend. XII with Amend. XX, Sec. 3 changes)

The Congress may determine the Time of choosing the Electors, and the Day on which they shall give their Votes; which Day shall be the same throughout the United States.

choosing

No Person except a natural born Citizen, or a Citizen of the United States, at the time of the Adoption of this Constitution, shall be eligible to the Office of President; neither shall any person be eligible to that Office who shall not have attained to the Age of thirty five Years, and been fourteen Years a Resident within the United States.

In case of the removal of the President from office or of his death or resignation, the Vice President shall become President.

The next four paragraphs are Amendment XXV

Whenever there is a vacancy in the office of the Vice President, the President shall nominate a Vice President who shall take office upon confirmation by a majority vote of both Houses of Congress.

Whenever the President transmits to the President pro tempore of the Senate and the Speaker of the House of Representatives his written declaration that he is unable to discharge the powers and duties of his office, and until he transmits to them a written declaration to the contrary, such powers and duties shall be discharged by the Vice President as Acting President.

Whenever the Vice President and a majority of either the principal officers of the executive departments or of such other body as Congress may by law provide, transmit to the President pro tempore of the Senate and the Speaker of the House of Representatives their written declaration that the President is unable to discharge the powers and duties of his office, the Vice President shall immediately assume the powers and duties of the office as Acting President. Thereafter, when the President transmits to the President pro tempore of the Senate and the Speaker of the House of Representatives his written declaration that no inability exists, he shall resume the powers and duties of his office unless the Vice President and a majority of either the principal officers of the executive department or of such other body as Congress may by law provide, transmit within four days to the President pro tempore of the Senate and the Speaker of the House of Representatives their written declaration that the President is unable to discharge the powers and duties of his office. Thereupon Congress shall decide the issue, assembling within forty-eight hours for that purpose if not in session. If the Congress, within twenty-one days after receipt of the latter written declaration, or, if Congress is not in session, within twenty-one days after Congress is required to assemble, determines by two-thirds vote of both Houses that the President is unable to discharge the powers and duties of his office, the Vice President shall continue to discharge the same as Acting President; otherwise, the President shall resume the powers and duties of his office. (This and the previous three paragraphs are Amend. XXV.)

The President shall, at stated Times, receive for his Services, a Compensation, which shall neither be increased nor diminished during the Period for which he shall have been elected, and he shall not receive within that Period any other Emolument from the United States, or any of them.

Before he enter on the Execution of his Office, he shall take the following Oath or Affirmation:--"I do solemnly swear (or affirm) that I will faithfully execute the Office of President of the United States, and will to the best of my Ability, preserve, protect and defend the Constitution of the United States."

Section. 2. The President shall be Commander in Chief of the Army and Navy of the United States, and of the Militia of the several States, when called into the actual Service of the United States; he may require the Opinion, in writing, of the principal Officer in each of the executive Departments, upon any Subject relating to the Duties of their respective Offices, and he shall have Power to grant Reprieves and Pardons for Offenses against the United States, except in Cases of Impeachment.

He shall have Power, by and with the Advice and Consent of the Senate, to make Treaties, provided two thirds of the Senators present concur; and he shall nominate, and by and with the Advice and Consent of the Senate, shall appoint Ambassadors, other public Ministers and Consuls, Judges of the supreme Court, and all other Officers of the United States, whose Appointments are not herein otherwise provided for, and which shall be established by Law: but the Congress may by Law vest the Appointment of such inferior Officers, as they think proper, in the President alone, in the Courts of Law, or in the Heads of Departments.

The President shall have Power to fill up all Vacancies that may happen during the Recess of the Senate, by granting Commissions which shall expire at the End of their next Session.

Section. 3. He shall from time to time give to the Congress Information of the State of the Union, and recommend to their Consideration such Measures as he shall judge necessary and expedient; he may, on extraordinary Occasions, convene both Houses, or either of them, and in Case of Disagreement between them, with Respect to the Time of Adjournment, he may adjourn them to such Time as he shall think proper; he shall receive Ambassadors and other public Ministers; he shall take Care that the Laws be faithfully executed, and shall Commission all the Officers of the United States.

Section. 4. The President, Vice President and all civil Officers of the United States, shall be removed from Office on Impeachment for, and Conviction of, Treason, Bribery, or other high Crimes and Misdemeanors.

# ARTICLE III: THE JUDICIARY

Section. 1. The judicial Power of the United States, shall be vested in one supreme Court, and in such inferior Courts as the Congress may from time to time ordain and establish. The Judges, both of the supreme and inferior Courts, shall hold their Offices during good Behavior, and shall, at stated Times, receive for their Services, a Compensation, which shall not be diminished during their Continuance in Office.

Title added

Behavior

Section. 2. The judicial Power shall extend to all Cases, in Law and Equity, arising under this Constitution, the Laws of the United States, and Treaties made, or which shall be made, under their Authority;--to all Cases affecting Ambassadors, other public Ministers and Consuls;-- to all Cases of admiralty and maritime Jurisdiction;--to Controversies to which the United States shall be a Party;--to Controversies between two or more States;-- between Citizens of different States,-- between Citizens of the same State claiming Lands under Grants of different States,--but the Judicial power of the United States shall not be construed to extend to any suit in law or equity, commenced or prosecuted against one of the United States by Citizens of another State, or by Citizens or Subjects of any Foreign State. (Last clause is Amend. XI)

Two clauses deleted
< Amendment XI added

In all Cases affecting Ambassadors, other public Ministers and Consuls, and those in which a State shall be Party, the supreme Court shall have original Jurisdiction. In all the other Cases before mentioned, the supreme Court shall have appellate Jurisdiction, both as to Law and Fact, with such Exceptions, and under such Regulations as the Congress shall make.

The Trial of all Crimes, except in Cases of Impeachment; shall be by Jury; and such Trial shall be held in the State where the said Crimes shall have been committed; but when not committed within any State, the Trial shall be at such Place or Places as the Congress may by Law have directed.

Section. 3. Treason against the United States, shall consist only in levying War against them, or in adhering to their Enemies, giving them Aid and Comfort. No Person shall be convicted of Treason unless on the Testimony of two Witnesses to the same overt Act, or on Confession in open Court.

The Congress shall have Power to declare the Punishment of Treason, but no Attainder of Treason shall work Corruption of Blood, or Forfeiture except during the Life of the Person attainted.

No person shall be a Senator or Representative in Congress, or elector of President and Vice President, or hold any office, civil or military, under the United States, or under any State, who, having previously taken an oath, as a member of Congress, or as an officer of the United States, or as a member of any State legislature, or as an executive or judicial officer of any State, to support the Constitution of the United States, shall have engaged in insurrection or rebellion against the same, or given aid or comfort to the enemies thereof. But Congress may by a vote of two-thirds of each House, remove such disability. (Sec. 3, Amend. XIV)

This paragraph is Sec. 3, Amend. XIV

## ARTICLE IV: STATE STANDARDS

Title added

Section. 1. Full Faith and Credit shall be given in each State to the public Acts, Records, and judicial Proceedings of every other State; And the Congress may by general Laws prescribe the Manner in which such Acts, Records and Proceedings shall be proved, and the Effect thereof.

Section. 2. The Citizens of each State shall be entitled to all Privileges and Immunities of Citizens in the several States.

The right of citizens of the United States to vote shall not be denied or abridged by the United States or by any State on account of race or color.(Amend. XV)

<<Amendment XV added and short phrase and Sec. 2 deleted

A Person charged in any State with Treason, Felony, or other Crime, who shall flee from Justice, and be found in another State, shall on Demand of the executive Authority of the State from which he fled, be delivered up, to be removed to the State having Jurisdiction of the Crime.

Neither slavery nor involuntary servitude, except as a punishment for crime whereof the party shall have been duly convicted, shall exist within the United States, or any place subject to their jurisdiction.

Paragraph changed by Amend. XIII

All persons born or naturalized in the United States and subject to the jurisdiction thereof, are citizens of the United States and of the State wherein they reside. No State shall make or enforce any law which shall abridge the privileges or immunities of citizens of the United States; nor shall any State deprive any person of life, liberty, or property, without due process of law; nor deny to any person within its jurisdiction the equal protection of the laws.

<<Section 1, Amendment XIV added

Section. 3. New States may be admitted by the Congress into this Union; but no new State shall be formed or erected within the Jurisdiction of any other State; nor any State be formed by the Junction of two or more States, or Parts of States, without the Consent of the Legislatures of the States concerned as well as of the Congress.

The Congress shall have Power to dispose of and make all needful Rules and Regulations respecting the Territory or other Property belonging to the United States; and nothing in this Constitution shall be so construed as to Prejudice any Claims of the United States, or of any particular State.

Section. 4. The United States shall guarantee to every State in this Union a Republican Form of Government, and shall protect each of them against Invasion; and on Application of the Legislature, or of the Executive (when the Legislature cannot be convened) against domestic Violence.

## ARTICLE V: AMENDMENT METHODS

| | |
|---|---|
| The Congress, whenever two thirds of both Houses shall deem it necessary, shall propose Amendments to this Constitution, or, on the Application of the Legislatures of two thirds of the several States, shall call a Convention for proposing Amendments, which, in either Case, shall be valid to all Intents and Purposes, as Part of this Constitution, when ratified by the Legislatures of three fourths of the several States, or by Conventions in three fourths thereof, as the one or the other Mode of Ratification may be proposed by the Congress; and that no State, without its Consent, shall be deprived of it's equal Suffrage in the Senate. | Title added<br><br><br><br><br><br>Phrase: "Provided--- Article;" deleted<br>UPOOE |
| Congress shall have power to enforce amendments by appropriate legislation. (Sec. 2, Amend. XIII) | Sec. 2, Amend. XIII added |
| Amendments shall be inoperative unless it shall have been ratified as an amendment to the Constitution by the legislatures of three-fourths of the several States within seven years from the date of its submission to the States by the Congress. (Sec. 2, Amend. XXII) | Sec. 2, Amend. XXII added.<br>The words "this article" have been replaced by the word "amendments" in both cases above. |

# ARTICLE VI: DEBTS, SUPREME LAW, OATHS

All Debts contracted and Engagements entered into, before the Adoption of this Constitution, shall be as valid against the United States under this Constitution.

The validity of the public debt of the United States, authorized by law, including debts incurred for payment of pensions and bounties for services in suppressing insurrection or rebellion, shall not be questioned. But neither the United States nor any State shall assume or pay any debt or obligation incurred in aid of insurrection or rebellion against the United States; but all such debts, obligations and claims shall be held illegal and void. (Sec. 4, Amend. XIV)

| |
|---|
| Title added |
| Last phrase deleted UPOOE |
| Sec. 4, Amend. XIV added with slavery phrase deleted UAE |

This Constitution, and the Laws of the United States which shall be made in Pursuance thereof; and all Treaties made, or which shall be made, under the Authority of the United States, shall be the supreme Law of the Land; and the Judges in every State shall be bound thereby, any Thing in the Constitution or Laws of any State to the Contrary notwithstanding.

The Senators and Representatives before mentioned, and the Members of the several State Legislatures, and all executive and judicial Officers, both of the United States and of the several States, shall be bound by Oath or Affirmation, to support this Constitution; but no religious Test shall ever be required as a Qualification to any Office or public Trust under the United States.

# ARTICLE VII: RATIFICATION

The Ratification of the Conventions of three-fourths of the States, shall be sufficient for the Establishment of this Constitution between the States so ratifying the Same.

Done in Convention by Consent of the States ----

| |
|---|
| Title added |
| Word "nine" replaced with "three-fourths of the" UPOOE |
| Paragraph mostly deleted , UPOOE |

Note: This concludes incorporation of the Amendments and deletion of unnecessary verbiage. The basic meaning of the Constitution has not been changed at this point.

# CHAPTER THREE: MINOR CHANGES FOR MODERN CONDITIONS

Using the Chapter 2 format, this chapter argues for some minor and obvious changes. These changes are then incorporated, using *italics*, into the appropriate paragraphs to show how they read. To save space and paper the incorporation of these paragraphs do not appear in the complete document until the end of Chapter 4, along with the changes of that chapter. Items changed are as follows:

1.  Fifth Right (Amend. V):

 Old first sentence: … in cases arising in the land or naval forces, or in the Militia, when in actual service ….

New: …in cases arising in the *armed forces,* or in the Militia *(including the National Guard and Reserves),* when in actual service ….

Justification:  Modern nomenclature.

2.  Sixth Right (Amend. VI):

Old first sentence:  ….the accused shall enjoy the right to a speedy and public trial, by an impartial jury ….

New:  … the accused shall enjoy the right to a *public trial within six months (one year on appeal) of the date of arrest,* by an impartial jury ….

Justification:  Obviously being violated by Justice Department and States

3.  Seventh Right (Amend. VII):

Old first sentence:  …where the value in controversy shall exceed twenty dollars, the right of trial by jury ….

New:  …. where the value in controversy *exceeds one billionth of the nation's previous year's real GDP,* the right of trial by jury …..

Justification:  Plainly a constitution misstep and needs modern indexing.  The number recommended turns out to be approximately twelve thousand dollars (2009).

4.  Article I, Section 2, Paragraph 3:

Old paragraph:  The actual Enumeration shall be made within three Years after the fist Meeting of the Congress of the United States, and within every subsequent Term of ten Years, in such Manner as they shall by Law direct.  The number of Representatives shall not exceed one for every thirty Thousand, but each State shall have at Least one Representative.

New paragraph: The actual *population* Enumeration *(census) shall be made every ten years as the Congress* shall by Law direct. The number of Representatives shall not exceed one for every *four hundred* Thousand, but ….

Justification: The initial census requirement is no longer necessary and the number of citizens per representative needs to be more realistic. This paragraph could use further consideration for citizens need better intermediate representation.

5. Article I, Section 8, Duty 4:

Old paragraph: To coin Money, regulate the Value thereof, ….

New paragraph: To coin Money *and issue certificates of legal tender,* regulate the Value thereof, ….

Justification: Already being done. Makes Constitution more honest.

6. Article I, Section 8, Duty 6:

Old paragraph: To establish Post Offices and post Roads;

New paragraph: To establish Post Offices, post Roads, *interstate highways and waterways;*

Justification: Already being done.

7. Article I, Section 8, Duty 11:

Old paragraph: To raise and support Armies, but no Appropriation of Money to that Use shall be for a longer Term than two Years;

New paragraph: To raise and support *Armed Forces*, but no Appropriation of Money to that Use shall be for a longer Term than two Years *with exceptions* for *sophisticated weapon systems provided a detailed engineering and cost estimate for research, development and production are approved*;

Justification: Modern terminology. Complicated weapon systems have long development times. Extended contracts are already being done. (Note: Congress often meddles in the contract process driving the cost much higher)

8. Article I, Section 8, Duty 12:

Old paragraph: To provide and maintain a Navy;

New paragraph: To provide and maintain a Navy, *Air Force, Coast Guard and Space Program;*

Justification: Reality modernizations.

9. Article I, Section 8, Duty 13:

Old paragraph: To make Rules for the Government and Regulation of the land and naval Forces;

New paragraph: To make Rules for the Government and Regulation of the *Armed* Forces;

Justification: Modern nomenclature.

10. Article I, Section 8, Duty 16:

Old paragraph, last clause: …for the Erection of Forts, Magazines, Arsenals, dock-Yards and other needful Buildings;--And

New paragraph, last clause: …for the Erection of *Bases, Posts, Ports,* Arsenals and other needful Buildings;--And

Justification: Modernize terminology.

11. Article I, Section 10:

Old mid paragraph: …coin Money; emit Bills of Credit; make any Thing but gold and silver Coin a Tender in Payment of Debts; ….

New mid paragraph: …coin Money; *issue certificates of legal tender for* Payment of Debts; ….

Justification: More realistic.

12  Article II, Section 2, line 1:

Old line: The President shall be Commander in Chief of the Army and Navy ….

New line: The President shall be Commander in Chief of the *Armed Forces* ….

Justification: Modern terminology.

Inclusion of the above minor and modernizing changes will be made in the next complete reproduction of the Constitution at the end of Chapter 4.

# CHAPTER FOUR:   GENERALLY  ACCEPTED CHANGES

## PART  I :  THE PROS AND CONS

The changes in this chapter are those of the popular will or changes all Americans can reasonably believe in.   The plan is to make reasonable restrictions on the federal government, but not so restrictive as to be completely inflexible—otherwise amendments will be frequently needed.   Plus, changes should not be so non-libertarian that a large portion of the common citizens or middle class will not be willing to obey the change (e.g., like prohibition).

For this chapter I've used Table 2 from Chapter 1, Part 5B, as well as the items supported by public surveys mentioned in either book reference two or five or both.[27] Other items supported by public survey but not included here are: the Equal Rights Amendment (ERA), national referendums, school prayer, regional primaries and free TV advertising.   Six common items have been chosen plus a favorite of the author--ethics.

1. Lengthening House Terms
2. Term Limits for Congress
3. War Powers and Continuity
4. Campaign Finance
5. Judicial Retirement
6. Balanced Budget
7. Ethics

When I say generally accepted, I'm speaking of the public.   Congresspersons are against any changes that decrease their power or that makes it more difficult to get elected.   Items two, four and six fall into this category.   The literature lists numerous pros and cons on all these subjects and since the areas already have quasi-approval of the people my reviews will be limited. Still, one must keep in mind that the literature is mostly written by liberal authors.   As you read the discussions of each item below, you may want to thumb forward to the corresponding recommended language in Part 2 of this chapter.

ITEM 1: HOUSE TERMS

Consensus has it for changing from two to four years with still a few calls for three years.   Some of the Founders even favored a one-year term in order for the representative to be "closer to the people."   Others, such as Madison, preferred three years.    The Founders finally compromised on the two-year term presently used.   That was then.[28] This is now and the world is a lot more complicated.   First let us look at the positive side of a four-year term change.

---

[27] Robinson (CSS), p.287;  and Sabato, p.182
[28] See Appendix 1; A Culture Comparison

PROS: 1) The representative has more time to learn the job and get comfortable with procedures and colleagues.
2) A greater amount of time is available for legislating versus campaigning.
3) More attention can be given to "national" versus "state" affairs.
4) There will be an increased willingness to tackle controversial topics.
5) Our technological world requires more experience.
6) Of all the world's republics, our representatives' terms are the shortest.

CONS: 1) It takes longer to remove a bad choice.
2) Too much power may be added to the President's party.
3) Representatives should be close to their constituents as the Founders suggested.

Present and past representatives are not in great disagreement with a longer term, but they do have problems with the timing of elections if a change is made. The options for this consideration are:

1) Hold the election coincident with that for the President every four years.
2) Stagger terms with one-half of the representatives elected every two years.
3) Use the same year as the President's election, but use a different month or day.
4) Stagger with one-forth every year.
5) Elect all representatives mid-way between Presidential elections.

Option one gives the President and his party more power, reducing the checks and balances of our system. Option three has a similar disadvantage. Options two and four complicate the system so the author will use option five which enhances the likelihood of a larger off-year voter participation.

ITEM 2: TERM LIMITS

Congresspersons obviously will not like this change as an amendment or otherwise. Term limits is certainly not a new topic and a Web page about the subject has been around for several years.[29] The pros and cons are as follows:

PROS: 1) Corruption is less likely; a major consideration.[30]
2) More attention will be paid to "national" interests instead of earmarks.
3) The country would get a younger Congress with new ideas.
4) Similar logic applied to Amendment XXII, for the President.
5) There is less incumbency advantage.

---

[29] Term Limits Web Site: http://termlimits.org; Retrieved (Retr.), 5 Sept 09.
[30] Mayhew, David R., *Divided We Govern,* Yale Univ. Press, 1991/2005, chap. 2.

CONS:  1)  Limits experience.
2) Civil servants and military brass gain power.[31]
3) The whole idea is anti-democratic.

The most common limit expressed for both houses is twelve years.  References generally do not discuss rerunning after sitting out one term or running for the other House after a short sit-out period. For a patriotic leader with determination to serve, I see no problem with either of these options.


ITEM 3:  WAR POWERS AND CONTINUIITY

As an Air Force engineering officer I had the pleasure of working with both the engineering and field operation personnel of our nation's intercontinental ballistic missiles (ICBMs), also known today as one of the weapons of mass destruction (WMD). The launch control facilities of these awesome weapons always had two launch officers who had to function together with the appropriate secret codes to launch a nuclear missile.  Our President, on the other hand, has sole control to initiate such destructive war, start World War III, and probably destroy civilization, as we know it.

The Founders obviously never envisioned the modern aspects of war or WMD.  If another finger is to be close to the red button, whose digit should it be—the Vice President, the Secretary of Defense, or someone of the Congresses' choosing? In addition, the President has taken or been given near dictatorial powers in several wars or military actions without a specific declaration by Congress as required by the Constitution.  More congressional control in this area is necessary, even if the executive is adamantly against it.

The War Powers Resolution Act of 1973, a result of the Vietnam War, is controversial at best and Presidents have pretty well ignored it on constitutional grounds. The Supreme Court has yet to make a reasonable interpretation of the Act.  Military actions, short of an all out maximum war effort, continue unabated as the U.S. attempts to be the world's policeman while nation building in our successful capitalistic image.  A worthy goal, but difficult to muster either in will power or purse. The idea here is to limit Presidential power for starting small wars or approving extensive covert actions without at least partial Congress approval.  The change recommended has firm support from both Congress and the public.

Progressing to the continuity factor, the Constitution has no directions as to how to fill the House seats in case of a successful WMD attack against our legislators.  This is an easy fix if handled as with Senator replacement.

---

[31] Hardin, Charles M., *Presidential Power and Accountability*, Univ. of Chicago Press, 1974. ( Liberal Professor Hardin devotes three chapters to the power of these bureaucracies)

PRO: 1) A world with WMD is extremely dangerous.
2) Some secrecy is required.
3) The War Powers Act is too flexible to restrain the President.
4) Fast decisions and action cannot wait for a congressional vote.
5) House continuity is essential and vacancies must be swiftly filled.

CON: 1) Founders intended Congress to have war power.
2) Too much secrecy is dangerous and despotic.
3) Executives are prone to wars.
4) Congress tends to relinquish power to Presidents in a crisis.
5) President's power may be overly limited.

Given the fact that the Secretary of Defense is probably best informed as to a military crisis situation, along with the Chairman of the Joint Chiefs of Staff, one of these officials should concur with the President for any nuclear response. If Washington, DC, is flattened, then responsibility must be transferred to the two top ranking military officers on the airborne command center, or the North American Aerospace Defense Command (NORAD), as it probably already is in some secret document. Beyond this, authority might be given to a combination of Governors from the larger States along with the top surviving general. An alternate Capitol should also be designated, such as Ellsworth Air Force Base in South Dakota. For now, I will just add a brief portion of the War Powers Act to the Constitution. (See Appendix 3 for Acts of interest)

ITEM 4: CAMPAIGN FINANCE

There are several laws that cover campaign finance and the subject has received more attention since the advent of television, the Internet, political action committees (PACs), and well sponsored lobbyists. The whole McCain-Feingold bill[32] cannot be put in a Constitution. That would violate our rule to keep the Constitution as short and straightforward as possible, so the language must be reduced to a paragraph or two and any numbers used indexed to some ongoing economic measure, such as the real gross domestic product (GDP). First, let us list the positive and negative aspects of the thesis:

PROS: 1) It reduces the incumbent advantage.
2) Public funding works for the President, why not Congresspersons?
3) Combats corruption
4) Campaigns are way too expensive.
5) TV sound bites are not thoughtful debate.
6) Candidates spend too much time and energy in money-raising efforts.
7) Lobbying influence is reduced.
8) Large contributions sway opinions and degrade trust.
9) PACs are too powerful.
10) Advertising goes primarily to the large swing states
11) Rich people would be unable to buy an office.

---

[32] See: http://en.wikipedia.org/wiki/Bipartisan_Campaign_Reform_Act, (Retr. 5 Sept 09).

12) There would be greater voter participation.

CONS: 1)  The Constitution guarantees freedom of speech.
2)  The media makes less money.
3)  Some lobbyists will be out of employment.
4)  Control is difficult, giving more power to the regulators such as the Federal Communications Commission (FCC) and Federal Election Commission (FEC).

Returning to the language problem, one of the easiest things to do is just ban PACs and lobbying contributions altogether and prohibit all TV except debates.  Note that the Supreme Court cannot prohibit campaign finance rules as a violation of the First Amendment if the prohibition is included in the Constitution.  This, of course, would be a contradiction, but the Constitution may require a few minor exceptions, as long as they are explained and justified.  The print media could be limited to résumés published at weekly intervals over a set pre-election period such as two or three months.  Brief language to cover this subject is difficult and some details must be left for Congress to police their own house.

## ITEM 5:  JUDICIARY RETIREMENT

This item correlates to item two that is also a term limit—a term limit of age.  Since the average death age varies over time with changes in health care, etc., it is probably best to index the retirement of judges with life expectancy data.

PROS: 1)  Judges do become sick, incompetent, and even senile.
2)  Some tend to become carried away with their importance, placing ego above country.
3)  They tend not to retire on their own, even with full pay at age 65.
4)  Their judgments are often either liberal or conservative depending on appointment timing.
5)  The Supreme Court "has" made legislative (activist) law changes.
6)  A younger court might take more cases.
7)  People did not live as long in the late 18th Century (e.g., longevity was in the mid forties).[33]

CONS: 1)  The Founders worried about political influence on salaries.
2)  Judges have a higher approval rating than Congress.
3)  Experience is critical.

This fix can easily be made in Article III of the Constitution.

---

[33]See Appendix 1.

ITEM 6: BALANCED BUDGET

Discussed for decades, a constitutional amendment to balance the budget has already been tried with 32 states proposing a single subject convention, two short of the two-thirds required. Congress members have introduced Balanced Budget Amendments (BBAs) numerous times, and they have even come close to passing on more than one occasion. Most authors, this one included, consider the budget and deficit to be grossly out of control. Congress baulks at fixing the problem because it affects their pork projects. A Deficit Control Act was actually passed once, but soon disregarded. Logically, proposed changes often have a safety outlet or valve of some type in case of grave security or economic difficulties. Heritage Foundation memo #580 points out that the language of most of the recommended amendments is too weak to be effective.[34] The seriousness of this subject needs more pros and cons than the other six topics of this chapter.

PROS: 1) The Senate increases House appropriations—when they should reduce them.
2) A principle topic of the Founders in the 1787 Convention was to pay the debts of the Revolution.
3) Relief can be phased in over several years.
4) For a good portion of the Republic there were no annual deficits (e.g., until the 1930s, excepting the Civil War).
5) Balanced budgets work fairly well in the States.
6) Emergency funding and borrowing can still be allowed.
7) The political process has yet to show it can solve the problem.
8) House members have retired in discuss and frustration over our budget and debt problems.
9) The earmark (pork) portion of the budget is particularly bad.
10) Omnibus bills also aggravate the problem.
11) Interest on the debt is the third largest federal expenditure.
12) It is unethical to transfer debt to children and grand children and it violates the Posterity Clause of the Constitution.
13) It is hard to organize support from unborn taxpayers.
14) Excessive budgets are a structural problem of the Constitution.
15) Better control over lobbying never happens.
16) President Reagan started cuts, but Congress stopped them.
17) The national debt is now in excess of 10 trillion dollars (mid 2009).
18) The Federal government will never cut entitlements.

CONS: 1) We should not clutter up our basic document with variable economic factors.
2) It would be troublesome to respond to emergencies.
3) Lawyers will find a loopholes.
4) The political process should be made to work; BB is not a fundamental law.
5) States sometimes need pork projects, but Congress is so busy it has no time to discuss them.

---

[34] Heritage Web Memo; http://www.heritage.org /Research/Budget/wm580.cfm; (Retr. 9/8/09).

6) Waiver clauses may not be sufficient.
7) States do not have serious defense requirements.
8) Supermajority override numbers are difficult to rationalize.
9) U.S. prosperity could be damaged.
10) In a recession or depression (as in 1930s or late 2000s) the federal government would be required to perform anti-recovery functions such as raising taxes, while an economic stimulus might actually help.
11) Enforcement would be difficult, giving more power to the regulatory agencies.

The pros outweigh the cons so insertion language includes time as well as dollar limitations. The danger of the country going into default is real and must be corrected.


ITEM 7: ETHICS

The references I have used gave little attention to this important part of operating a government. Sabato has a note on the subject and Sundquist discusses Congressional scandals briefly. Since one of the main reasons I wrote this book was the dalliance of President Clinton, and other politicians, I have included the topic here.

PROS: 1) We expect our leaders to set an example for citizens and our youth.
2) Clinton's impeachment acquittal was pure politics.
3) Fewer scandals will improve our government.
4) Religious leaders have not helped the situation.
5) Church attendance has decreased.
6) The two ethics Acts passed by Congress do not seem to help.
7) Scandals may lead to breaches in security.
8) The military might take over a scandal-ridden government.
9) The media, in general, has not condemned bad behavior.
10) The Roman Empire collapsed from moral decay.
11) The Founders assumed civil leadership would be honest.
12) The President, as chief of the Armed Forces, should be expected to live up to the ethics section of the Uniform Code of Military Justice (UCMJ).

CONS: 1) You cannot legislate morals and ethics.
2) Too error is human.
3) Corruption has been with us for ages.
4) Sexual transgressions are normal.
5) Honesty may be dangerous in foreign negotiations.

Contraire number one being true, the best we can probably do is to include an ethics statement in the oath of the President and other federal officers. At least then, the Senate will have a little more ammunition when impeachment occurs the next time.

## CHAPTER 4  PART 2:
## CREATING LANGUAGE TO INCLUDE THE SEVEN ITEMS
### (New words are underlined)

HOUSE TERMS LANGUAGE:  (Item 1)

Article I, Section 2: Present Language: "The House of Representatives shall be composed of Members chosen every second Year by the People...."

Change to:  The House of Representatives shall be composed of Members chosen midway between Presidential elections and every fourth Year by the People....

TERM LIMIT LANGUAGE:  (Item 2)

Article I, Section 1:  Add a second sentence.  No Congressperson shall serve more than twelve consecutive years.

WAR POWERS AND CONTINUITY LANGUAGE:  (Item 3)

Article II, Section 2:  Add this sentence at the end of paragraph one: In reacting to a Weapons of Mass Destruction (WMD) attack, the War Powers of the President are limited to an short immediate response prior to Congressional approval for further action. The launching of nuclear weapons requires approval of at least two people. Congress shall elect a three person council to monitor and approve ongoing covert actions. Approvals may be by secure electronic means.

Article I, Section 2:  For House continuity--add a sentence similar to clause 2, paragraph 2, and section 3 about Senate continuity; i.e., after sentence one of paragraph 4, section 2 add:  The legislature of any State may empower the ranking executive thereof to make temporary appointments until the people fill the vacancies by election as the legislature may direct. (And make the last sentence into a new paragraph)

Note:  I've left a little blank space occasionally for your comments.

CAMPAIGN FINANCE LANGUAGE:  (Item 4)

Article IV:  Add Section 5:  Pre-election media print for campaigning purposes are limited to 60 days prior to an election.  Video and audio campaigning of all types are limited to 30 days prior to an election and must contain multiple subjects debated on two or more sides with equal time. No organization of any type may donate more money than one billionth of the national real GDP of the previous year to any candidate or election cause. Individuals are limited to one-fourth the organizational amount.  This paragraph is the only exception to the Citizens' First Right (1st Amend.).

JUDICIAL RETIREMENT LANGUAGE:  (Item 5)

Article III, Section 1:  Revise the second sentence to read:  The Judges, both of the supreme and inferior Courts, shall hold their Offices during good Behavior, <u>but commence mandatory retirement at least one year prior to the statistical longevity age for his or her gender.</u>

Modify the last clause of Section 1 into a sentence to read:  <u>They</u> shall, at stated Times, receive....


BALANCED BUDGET LANGUAGE:  (Item 6)

Article VI:  Add new paragraph two:  <u>The Congress shall plan each year to balance the federal budget.  The planned expenditures shall not exceed 90 percent of the estimated revenues, nor will total borrowed funds exceed one-forth of the previous years real GDP. Actual expenditures larger than those budgeted will be reflected in a like percentage decrease in Congressional salaries until the budget is balanced.  Emergency exceptions require a two-thirds vote by both houses and concurrence of two-thirds of State Governors.  Without a formal declaration of war, emergency fund votes must be re-taken every three months.</u>


ETHICS LANGUAGE:  (Item 7)

Article II, Section 1, last paragraph:  Add at end of last sentence (oath):  ...defend the Constitution of the United States<u>, and to set an example of honesty, ethics and morality for our citizens.</u>"

Article VI, last paragraph:  Add words as underlined:  ...support this Constitution <u>and ethical behavior</u>; but no religious....


ADDITIONAL CHANGES:

To support the above language some administrative changes are necessary in the Constitution.  For example, an implementation time line is required, particularly for the balanced budget since Congress continues to over spend and borrow.  Secondly, the use of statistics needs a basis not controlled by the government.

Add new paragraph three to Article VI:  <u>After emergency expenditures, Congress shall by law incorporate methods to efficiently recover the balanced budget and deficit limit.  Such</u>

methods shall be accomplished with dispatch in two years or less for domestic disruptions and six years or less for major military actions and will include across-the-board reductions in expenditures in all areas without exception.

Add to paragraph three of Article I, Sec 2:  Every ten years the Congress shall appoint a commission of seven top economists from seven large universities in diverse geographic areas to study, and revise if necessary, the calculations and methodology of the economic statistics used by the federal government.

# CHAPTER 4 PART 3: INCORPORATING ACCEPTED CHANGES

## CONSTITUTION OF THE UNITED STATES
(Incorporates changes 1, 2, & 3)

## PREAMBLE:

We the People of the United States, in Order to form a more perfect Union, establish Justice, insure domestic Tranquility, provide for the common defense, promote the general Welfare, and secure the Blessings of Liberty to ourselves and our Posterity, do ordain and establish this Constitution for the United States of America.

## CITIZEN'S BILL OR RIGHTS:

First Right   (Amend. I). Congress shall make no law respecting an establishment of religion, or prohibiting the free exercise thereof; or abridging the freedom of speech, or of the press, or the right of the people peaceably to assemble, and to petition the Government for a redress of grievances.

Second Right   (Amend. II). A well regulated Militia, being necessary to the security of a free State, the right of the people to keep and bear Arms, shall not be infringed.

Third Right (Amend. III). No Soldier shall, in time of peace be quartered in any house, without the consent of the Owner, nor in time of war, but in a manner to be prescribed by law.

Fourth Right (Amend. IV). The right of the people to be secure in their persons, houses, papers, and effects, against unreasonable searches and seizures, shall not be violated, and no Warrants shall issue, but upon probable cause, supported by Oath or affirmation, and particularly describing the place to be searched, and the persons or things to be seized.

Fifth Right (Amend. V). No person shall be held to answer for a capital, or otherwise infamous crime, unless on a presentment or indictment of a Grand Jury, except in cases arising in the *armed* forces, or in the Militia *(including the National Guard and Reserves)*, when in actual service in time of War or public danger; nor shall any person be subject for the same offence to be twice put in jeopardy of life or limb, nor shall be compelled in any criminal case to be a witness against himself, nor be deprived of life, liberty, or property, without due process of law; nor shall private property be taken for public use without just compensation.

Sixth Right (Amend. VI). In all criminal prosecutions, the accused shall enjoy the right to a *public trial within six months (one year on appeal) of the date of arrest*, by an impartial jury of the State and district wherein the crime shall have been committed; which district shall have been previously ascertained by law, and to be informed of the nature and cause of the accusation; to be confronted with the witnesses against him; to have compulsory process for obtaining witnesses in his favor, and to have the assistance of counsel for his defense.

Seventh Right (Amend. VII). In Suits at common law, where the value in controversy *exceeds one billionth of the nation's previous year's real Gross Domestic Product (GDP)*, the right of trial by jury shall be preserved, and no fact tried by a jury shall be otherwise re-examined in any Court of the United States, than according to the rules of the common law.

Eighth Right (Amend. VIII). Excessive bail shall not be required, nor excessive fines imposed, nor cruel and unusual punishments inflicted.

Ninth Right (Amend. IX). The enumeration in the Constitution of certain rights shall not be construed to deny or disparage others retained by the people.

Tenth Right (Amend. X). The powers not delegated to the United States by the Constitution, nor prohibited by it to the States, are reserved to the States respectively, or to the people.

# ARTICLE I THE CONGRESS

Section. 1. All legislative Powers herein granted shall be vested in a Congress of the United States, which shall consist of a Senate and House of Representatives. <u>No Congressperson shall serve more than twelve consecutive years.</u>

Section. 2. The House of Representatives shall be composed of Members chosen <u>midway between Presidential elections and</u> every <u>fourth</u> Year by the People of the several States, and the Electors in each State shall have the Qualifications requisite for Electors of the most numerous Branch of the State Legislature. No Person shall be a Representative who shall not have attained to the Age of twenty five Years, and been seven Years a Citizen of the United States, and who shall not, when elected, be an Inhabitant of that State in which he shall be chosen.

Representatives shall be apportioned among the several States according to their respective numbers, counting the whole number of persons in each State, excluding Indians not taxed. But when the right to vote at any election for the choice of electors for President and Vice President of the United States, Representatives in Congress, the Executive and Judicial officers of a State, or the members of the Legislature thereof, is denied to any of the male inhabitants of such State, being twenty-one years of age, and citizens of the United States, or in any way abridged, except for participation in rebellion, or other crime, the basis of representation therein shall be reduced in the proportion which the number of such male citizens shall bear to the whole number of male citizens twenty-one years of age in such State. (Sec. 2, Amend. XIV)

The actual *population* Enumeration *(census) shall be made every ten years as the Congress* shall by Law direct. The number of Representatives shall not exceed one for every *four hundred* Thousand, but each State shall have at Least one Representative. Every ten years the Congress shall appoint a commission of seven top economists from seven large universities in diverse geographic areas to study, and revise if necessary, the calculations and methodology of the economic statistics used by the federal government.

When vacancies happen in the Representation from any State, the Executive Authority thereof shall issue Writs of Election to fill such Vacancies. The legislature of any State may empower the ranking executive thereof to make temporary appointments until the people fill the vacancies by election as the legislature may direct.

The House of Representatives shall choose their Speaker and other Officers; and shall have the sole Power of Impeachment.


Section. 3. The Senate of the United States shall be composed of two Senators from each State, elected by the people thereof, for six years; and each Senator shall have one vote. The electors in each State shall have the qualifications requisite for electors of the most numerous branches of the State legislatures.

Senators shall be divided as equally as may be into three Classes, so that one third may be chosen every second Year.

When vacancies happen in the representation of any State in the Senate, the executive authority of such State shall issue writs of election to fill such vacancies: Provided, That the legislature of any State may empower the executive thereof to make temporary appointments until the people fill the vacancies by election as the legislature may direct.

No Person shall be a Senator who shall not have attained to the Age of thirty Years, and been nine Years a Citizen of the United States, and who shall not, when elected, be an Inhabitant of that State for which he shall be chosen.

The Vice President of the United States shall be President of the Senate, but shall have no Vote, unless they be equally divided.

The Senate shall choose their other Officers, and also a President pro tempore, in the Absence of the Vice President, or when he shall exercise the Office of President of the United States.

The Senate shall have the sole Power to try all Impeachments. When sitting for that Purpose, they shall be on Oath or Affirmation. When the President of the United States is tried, the Chief Justice shall preside: And no Person shall be convicted without the Concurrence of two thirds of the Members present.

Judgment in Cases of Impeachment shall not extend further than to removal from Office, and disqualification to hold and enjoy any Office of honor, Trust or Profit under the United States: but the Party convicted shall nevertheless be liable and subject to Indictment, Trial, Judgment and Punishment, according to Law.

Section. 4. The Times, Places and Manner of holding Elections for Senators and Representatives, shall be prescribed in each State by the Legislature thereof; but the Congress may at any time by Law make or alter such Regulations, except as to the Places of choosing Senators.

The terms of the Senators and Representatives shall end at noon on the 3d day of January. (Clause 2, Sec. 1, Amend. XX)

The Congress shall assemble at least once in every year, and such meeting shall begin at noon on the 3d day of January, unless they shall by law appoint a different day. (Sec. 2, Amend. XX)

Section. 5. Each House shall be the Judge of the Elections, Returns and Qualifications of its own Members, and a Majority of each shall constitute a Quorum to do Business; but a smaller Number may adjourn from day to day, and may be authorized to compel the Attendance of absent Members, in such Manner, and under such Penalties as each House may provide.

Each House may determine the Rules of its Proceedings, punish its Members for disorderly Behavior, and, with the Concurrence of two thirds, expel a Member.

Each House shall keep a Journal of its Proceedings, and from time to time publish the same, excepting such Parts as may in their Judgment require Secrecy; and the Yeas and Nays of the Members of either House on any question shall, at the Desire of one fifth of those Present, be entered on the Journal.

Neither House, during the Session of Congress, shall, without the Consent of the other, adjourn for more than three days, nor to any other Place than that in which the two Houses shall be sitting.

Section. 6. The Senators and Representatives shall receive a Compensation for their Services, to be ascertained by Law, and paid out of the Treasury of the United States.

No law, varying the compensation for the services of the Senators and Representatives, shall take effect, until an election of Representatives shall have intervened. (Amend. XXVII)

They shall in all Cases, except Treason, Felony and Breach of the Peace, be privileged from Arrest during their Attendance at the Session of their respective Houses, and in going to and returning from the same; and for any Speech or Debate in either House, they shall not be questioned in any other Place.

No Senator or Representative shall, during the Time for which he was elected, be appointed to any civil Office under the Authority of the United States, which shall have been created, or the Emoluments whereof shall have been increased during such time; and no Person holding any Office under the United States, shall be a Member of either House during his Continuance in Office.

Section. 7. All Bills for raising Revenue shall originate in the House of Representatives; but the Senate may propose or concur with Amendments as on other Bills. Every Bill which shall have passed the House of Representatives and the Senate, shall, before it becomes a Law, be presented to the President of the United States; If he approve he shall sign it, but if not he shall return it, with his Objections to that House in which it shall have originated, who shall enter the Objections at large on their Journal, and proceed to reconsider it. If after such Reconsideration two thirds of that House shall agree to pass the Bill, it shall be sent, together with the Objections, to the other House, by which it shall likewise be reconsidered, and if approved by two thirds of that House, it shall become a Law. But in all such Cases the Votes of both Houses shall be determined by yeas and Nays, and the Names of the Persons voting for and against the Bill shall be entered on the Journal of each House respectively. If any Bill shall not be returned by the President within ten Days (Sundays excepted) after it shall have been presented to him, the Same shall be a Law, in like Manner as if he had signed it, unless the Congress by their Adjournment prevent its Return, in which Case it shall not be a Law. Every Order, Resolution, or Vote to which the Concurrence of the Senate and House of Representatives may be necessary (except on a question of Adjournment) shall be presented to the President of the United States; and before the Same shall take Effect, shall be approved by him, or being disapproved by him, shall be re-passed by two thirds of the Senate and House of Representatives, according to the Rules and Limitations prescribed in the Case of a Bill.

Section. 8. The Congress shall have Power To lay and collect Taxes, Duties, Imposts and Excises, to pay the Debts and provide for the common Defense and general Welfare of the United States; but all Duties, Imposts and Excises shall be uniform throughout the United States;

To borrow Money on the credit of the United States;

To regulate Commerce with foreign Nations, and among the several States, and with the Indian Tribes;

To establish an uniform Rule of Naturalization, and uniform Laws on the subject of Bankruptcies throughout the United States;

To coin Money *and issue certificates of legal tender*, regulate the Value thereof, and of foreign Coin, and fix the Standard of Weights and Measures;

To provide for the Punishment of counterfeiting the Securities and current Coin of the United States;

To establish Post Offices and post Roads, *interstate highways and waterways;*

To promote the Progress of Science and useful Arts, by securing for limited Times to Authors and Inventors the exclusive Right to their respective Writings and Discoveries;

To constitute Tribunals inferior to the Supreme Court;

To define and punish Piracies and Felonies committed on the high Seas, and Offenses against the Law of Nations;

To declare War, grant Letters of Marque and Reprisal, and make Rules concerning Captures on Land and Water;

To raise and support *Armed Forces*, but no Appropriation of Money to that Use shall be for a longer Term than two Years *with exceptions for sophisticated weapon systems provided a detailed engineering and cost estimate for research, development and production are approved.*

To provide and maintain a Navy, *Air Force, Coast Guard, and Space Program;*

To make Rules for the Government and Regulation of the *Armed* Forces;

To provide for calling forth the Militia to execute the Laws of the Union, suppress Insurrections and repel Invasions;

To provide for organizing, arming, and disciplining, the Militia, and for governing such Part of them as may be employed in the Service of the United States, reserving to the States respectively, the Appointment of the Officers, and the Authority of training the Militia according to the discipline prescribed by Congress;

To exercise exclusive Legislation in all Cases whatsoever, over such District (not exceeding ten Miles square) as may, by Cession of particular States, and the Acceptance of Congress, become the Seat of the Government of the United States, and to exercise like Authority over all Places purchased by the Consent of the Legislature of the State in which the Same shall be, for the Erection of *Bases, Posts, Ports*, Arsenals, and other needful Buildings;--And

To make all Laws which shall be necessary and proper for carrying into Execution the foregoing Powers, and all other Powers vested by this Constitution in the Government of the United States or in any Department or Officer thereof.

Section. 9. The Privilege of the Writ of Habeas Corpus shall not be suspended, unless when in Cases of Rebellion or Invasion the public Safety may require it.

No Bill of Attainder or ex post facto Law shall be passed.

The Congress shall have power to lay and collect taxes on incomes, from whatever source derived, without apportionment among the several States, and without regard to any census or enumeration. (Amend. XVI)

No Capitation, or other direct, Tax shall be laid, unless in Proportion to the Census or Enumeration herein before directed to be taken.

No Tax or Duty shall be laid on Articles exported from any State.

No Preference shall be given by any Regulation of Commerce or Revenue to the Ports of one State over those of another: nor shall Vessels bound to, or from, one State, be obliged to enter, clear, or pay Duties in another.

No Money shall be drawn from the Treasury, but in Consequence of Appropriations made by Law; and a regular Statement and Account of the

Receipts and Expenditures of all public Money shall be published from time to     time.

No Title of Nobility shall be granted by the United States: And no Person holding any Office of Profit or Trust under them, shall, without the Consent of the Congress, accept of any present, Emolument, Office, or Title, of any kind whatever, from any King, Prince, or foreign State.

Section. 10. No State shall enter into any Treaty, Alliance, or Confederation; grant Letters of Marque and Reprisal; coin Money; *issue certificates of legal tender for* Payment of Debts; pass any Bill of Attainder, ex post facto Law, or Law impairing the Obligation of Contracts, or grant any Title of Nobility.

No State shall, without the Consent of the Congress, lay any Imposts or Duties on Imports or Exports, except what may be absolutely necessary for executing it's inspection Laws: and the net Produce of all Duties and Imposts, laid by any State on Imports or Exports, shall be for the Use of the Treasury of the United States; and all such Laws shall be subject to the Revision and Control of the Congress.

No State shall, without the Consent of Congress, lay any Duty of Tonnage, keep Troops, or Ships of War in time of Peace, enter into any Agreement or Compact with another State, or with a foreign Power, or engage in War, unless actually invaded, or in such imminent Danger as will not admit of delay.

## ARTICLE II THE EXECUTIVE.

Section. 1. The executive Power shall be vested in a President of the United States of America. He shall hold his Office during the Term of four Years, and, together with the Vice President, chosen for the same Term, be elected, as follows:

Each State shall appoint, in such Manner as the Legislature thereof may direct, a Number of Electors, equal to the whole Number of Senators and Representatives to which the State may be entitled in the Congress: but no Senator or Representative, or Person holding an Office of Trust or Profit under the United States, shall be appointed an Elector.

The Electors shall meet in their respective states, and vote by ballot for President and Vice President, one of whom, at least, shall not be an inhabitant of the same state with themselves; they shall name in their ballots the person voted for as President, and in distinct ballots the person voted for as Vice-President, and they shall make distinct lists of all persons voted for as President, and of all persons voted for as Vice-President, and of the number of votes for each, which lists they shall sign and certify, and transmit sealed to the seat of the government of the United States, directed to the President of the Senate;--The President of the Senate shall, in the presence of the Senate and House of Representatives, open all the certificates and the votes shall then be counted;--The person having the greatest number of votes for President, shall be the President, if such number be a majority of the whole number of Electors appointed; and if no person have such majority, then from the persons having the highest numbers not exceeding three on the list of those voted for as President, the House of Representatives shall choose immediately, by ballot, the President. But in choosing the President, the votes shall be taken by states, the representation from each state having one vote; a quorum for this purpose shall consist of a member or members from two-thirds of the states, and a majority of all the states shall be necessary to a choice.

If, at the time fixed for the beginning of the term of the President, the President elect shall have died, the Vice President elect shall become President. If a President shall not have been chosen before the time fixed for the beginning of his term, or if the President elect shall have failed to qualify, then the Vice President elect shall act as President until a President shall have qualified; and the Congress may by law provide for the case wherein neither a President elect nor a Vice President elect shall have qualified, declaring who shall then act as President, or the manner in which one who is to act shall be selected, and such person shall act accordingly until a President or Vice President shall have qualified. (Sec. 3, Amend. XX)

The person having the greatest number of votes as Vice-President, shall be the Vice-President, if such number be a majority of the whole number of Electors appointed, and if no person have a majority, then from the two highest numbers on the list, the Senate shall choose the Vice-President; a quorum for the purpose shall consist of two-thirds of the whole number of Senators, and a majority of the whole number shall be necessary to a choice. But no person constitutionally ineligible to the office of President shall be eligible to that of Vice-President of the United States. (Amend. XII with Amend. XX, Sec. 3 changes)


The Congress may determine the Time of choosing the Electors, and the Day on which they shall give their Votes; which Day shall be the same throughout the United States.

No Person except a natural born Citizen, or a Citizen of the United States, at the time of the Adoption of this Constitution, shall be eligible to the Office of President; neither shall any person be eligible to that Office who shall not have attained to the Age of thirty five Years, and been fourteen Years a Resident within the United States.

In case of the removal of the President from office or of his death or resignation, the Vice President shall become President.

Whenever there is a vacancy in the office of the Vice President, the President shall nominate a Vice President who shall take office upon confirmation by a majority vote of both Houses of Congress.

Whenever the President transmits to the President pro tempore of the Senate and the Speaker of the House of Representatives his written declaration that he is unable to discharge the powers and duties of his office, and until he transmits to them a written declaration to the contrary, such powers and duties shall be discharged by the Vice President as Acting President.

Whenever the Vice President and a majority of either the principal officers of the executive departments or of such other body as Congress may by law provide, transmit to the President pro tempore of the Senate and the Speaker of the House of Representatives their written declaration that the President is unable to discharge the powers and duties of his office, the Vice President shall immediately assume the powers and duties of the office as Acting President. Thereafter, when the President transmits to the President pro tempore of the Senate and the Speaker of the House of Representatives his written declaration that no inability exists, he shall resume the powers and duties of his office unless the Vice President and a majority of either the principal officers of the executive department or of such other body as Congress may by law provide, transmit within four days to the President pro tempore of the Senate and the Speaker of the House of Representatives their written declaration that the President is unable to discharge the powers and duties of his office. Thereupon Congress shall decide the issue, assembling within forty-eight hours for that purpose if not in session. If the Congress, within twenty-one days after receipt of the latter written declaration, or, if Congress is not in session, within twenty-one days after Congress is required to assemble, determines by two-thirds vote of both Houses that the President is unable to discharge the powers and duties of his office, the Vice President shall continue to discharge the same as Acting President; otherwise, the President shall resume the powers and duties of his office. (This and the previous three paragraphs are Amend. XXV)

The President shall, at stated Times, receive for his Services, a Compensation, which shall neither be increased nor diminished during the Period for which he shall have been elected, and he shall not receive within that Period any other Emolument from the United States, or any of them.

Before he enter on the Execution of his Office, he shall take the following Oath or Affirmation:--"I do solemnly swear (or affirm) that I will faithfully execute the Office of President of the United States, and will to the best of my Ability, preserve, protect and defend the Constitution of the United States, and to set an example of honesty, ethics and morality for our citizens."

Section. 2. The President shall be Commander in Chief of the *Armed Forces* of the United States, and of the Militia of the several States, when called into the actual Service of the United States; he may require the Opinion, in writing, of the principal Officer in each of the executive Departments, upon any Subject relating to the Duties of their respective Offices, and he shall have Power to grant Reprieves and Pardons for Offenses against the United States, except in Cases of Impeachment. In reacting to a Weapons of Mass Destruction (WMD) attack, the War Powers of the President are limited to a short immediate response prior to Congressional approval for further action. The launching of nuclear weapons requires approval of at least two people. Congress shall elect a three person council to monitor and approve ongoing covert actions. Approvals may be by secure electronic means.

He shall have Power, by and with the Advice and Consent of the Senate, to make Treaties, provided two thirds of the Senators present concur; and he shall nominate, and by and with the Advice and Consent of the Senate, shall appoint Ambassadors, other public Ministers and Consuls, Judges of the supreme Court, and all other Officers of the United States, whose Appointments are not herein otherwise provided for, and which shall be established by Law: but the Congress may by Law vest the Appointment of such inferior Officers, as they think proper, in the President alone, in the Courts of Law, or in the Heads of Departments.

The President shall have Power to fill up all Vacancies that may happen during the Recess of the Senate, by granting Commissions, which shall expire at the End of their next Session.

Section. 3. He shall from time to time give to the Congress Information of the State of the Union, and recommend to their Consideration such Measures as he shall judge necessary and expedient; he may, on extraordinary Occasions, convene both Houses, or either of them, and in Case of Disagreement between them, with Respect to the Time of Adjournment, he may adjourn them to such Time as he shall think proper; he shall receive Ambassadors and other public Ministers; he shall take Care that the Laws be faithfully executed, and shall Commission all the Officers of the United States.

Section. 4. The President, Vice President and all civil Officers of the United States, shall be removed from Office on Impeachment for, and Conviction of, Treason, Bribery, or other high Crimes and Misdemeanors.

## ARTICLE. III  THE JUDICIARY

Section. 1. The judicial Power of the United States shall be vested in one Supreme Court, and in such inferior Courts as the Congress may from time to time ordain and establish. The Judges, both of the supreme and inferior Courts, shall hold their Offices during good Behavior, but commence mandatory retirement at least one year prior to the statistical longevity age for his or her gender.  They shall, at stated Times, receive for their Services, a Compensation, which shall not be diminished during their Continuance in Office.

Section. 2. The judicial Power shall extend to all Cases, in Law and Equity, arising under this Constitution, the Laws of the United States, and Treaties made, or which shall be made, under their Authority;--to all Cases affecting Ambassadors, other public Ministers and Consuls;-- to all Cases of admiralty and maritime Jurisdiction;--to Controversies to which the United States shall be a Party;--to Controversies between two or more States;-- between Citizens of different States,-- between Citizens of the same State claiming Lands under Grants of different States,--but the Judicial power of the United States shall not be construed to extend to any suit in law or equity, commenced or prosecuted against one of the United States by Citizens of another State, or by Citizens or Subjects of any Foreign State. (Last clause is Amend. XI)

In all Cases affecting Ambassadors, other public Ministers and Consuls, and those in which a State shall be Party, the supreme Court shall have original Jurisdiction. In all the other Cases before mentioned, the supreme Court shall have appellate Jurisdiction, both as to Law and Fact, with such Exceptions, and under such Regulations as the Congress shall make.

The Trial of all Crimes, except in Cases of Impeachment; shall be by Jury; and such Trial shall be held in the State where the said Crimes shall have been committed; but when not committed within any State, the Trial shall be at such Place or Places as the Congress may by Law have directed.

Section. 3. Treason against the United States, shall consist only in levying War against them, or in adhering to their Enemies, giving them Aid and Comfort. No Person shall be convicted of Treason unless on the Testimony of two Witnesses to the same overt Act, or on Confession in open Court.

The Congress shall have Power to declare the Punishment of Treason, but no Attainder of Treason shall work Corruption of Blood, or Forfeiture except during the Life of the Person attainted.

No person shall be a Senator or Representative in Congress, or elector of President and Vice President, or hold any office, civil or military, under the United States, or under any State, who, having previously taken an oath, as a member of Congress, or as an officer of the United States, or as a member of any State legislature, or as an executive or judicial officer of any State, to support the Constitution of the United States, shall have engaged in insurrection or rebellion against the same, or given aid or comfort to the enemies thereof. But Congress may by a vote of two-thirds of each House, remove such disability.

## ARTICLE. IV  STATE STANDARDS

Section. 1. Full Faith and Credit shall be given in each State to the public Acts, Records, and judicial Proceedings of every other State; And the Congress may by general Laws prescribe the Manner in which such Acts, Records and Proceedings shall be proved, and the Effect thereof.

Section. 2. The Citizens of each State shall be entitled to all Privileges and Immunities of Citizens in the several States.

The right of citizens of the United States to vote shall not be denied or abridged by the United States or by any State on account of race, or color. (Amend. XV)

A Person charged in any State with Treason, Felony, or other Crime, who shall flee from Justice, and be found in another State, shall on Demand of the executive Authority of the State from which he fled, be delivered up, to be removed to the State having Jurisdiction of the Crime.

Neither slavery nor involuntary servitude, except as a punishment for crime whereof the party shall have been duly convicted, shall exist within the United States, or any place subject to their jurisdiction.

All persons born or naturalized in the United States and subject to the jurisdiction thereof, are citizens of the United States and of the State wherein they reside. No State shall make or enforce any law which shall abridge the privileges or immunities of citizens of the United States; nor shall any State deprive any person of life, liberty, or property, without due process of law; nor deny to any person within its jurisdiction the equal protection of the laws.

Section. 3. New States may be admitted by the Congress into this Union; but no new State shall be formed or erected within the Jurisdiction of any other State; nor any State be formed by the Junction of two or more States, or Parts of States, without the Consent of the Legislatures of the States concerned as well as of the Congress.

The Congress shall have Power to dispose of and make all needful Rules and Regulations respecting the Territory or other Property belonging to the United States; and nothing in this Constitution shall be so construed as to Prejudice any Claims of the United States, or of any particular State.

Section. 4. The United States shall guarantee to every State in this Union a Republican Form of Government, and shall protect each of them against Invasion; and on Application of the Legislature, or of the Executive (when the Legislature cannot be convened) against domestic Violence

Section 5.  Pre-election media print for campaigning purposes are limited to 60 days prior to an election.  Video and audio campaigning of all types are limited to 30 days prior to an election and must contain multiple subjects debated on two or more sides with equal time.  No organization of any type may donate more money than one billionth of the national real GDP of the previous year to any candidate or election cause.  Individuals are limited to one-fourth the organizational amount.  This paragraph is the only exception to the Citizens First Right (1st Amend.).

## ARTICLE. V  AMENDMENT METHODS

The Congress, whenever two thirds of both Houses shall deem it necessary, shall propose Amendments to this Constitution, or, on the Application of the Legislatures of two thirds of the several States, shall call a Convention for proposing Amendments, which, in either Case, shall be valid to all Intents and Purposes, as Part of this Constitution, when ratified by the Legislatures of three fourths of the several States, or by Conventions in three fourths thereof, as the one or the other Mode of Ratification may be proposed by the Congress; and that no State, without its Consent, shall be deprived of it's equal Suffrage in the Senate.

Congress shall have power to enforce amendments by appropriate legislation. (Sec. 2, Amend. XIII)

Amendments shall be inoperative unless it shall have been ratified as an amendment to the Constitution by the legislatures of three-fourths of the several States within seven years from the date of its submission to the States by the Congress. (Sec. 2, Amend. XXII)

## ARTICLE VI  DEBTS, SUPREME LAW, OATHS

All Debts contracted and Engagements entered into, before the Adoption of this Constitution, shall be as valid against the United States under this Constitution.

The Congress shall plan each year to balance the federal budget. The planned expenditures shall not exceed 90 percent of the estimated revenues, nor will the total borrowed funds exceed one-forth of the previous years real GDP. Actual expenditures larger than those budgeted will be reflected in a like percentage decrease in Congressional salaries until the budget is balanced. Emergency exceptions require a two-thirds vote by both houses and concurrence of two-thirds of State Governors. Without a formal declaration of war, emergency fund votes must be re-taken every three months.

After emergency expenditures, Congress shall by law incorporate methods to efficiently recover the balanced budget and deficit limit. Such methods shall be accomplished with dispatch in two years or less for domestic disruptions and six years or less for major military actions and will include across-the-board reductions in expenditures in all areas without exception.

The validity of the public debt of the United States, authorized by law, including debts incurred for payment of pensions and bounties for services in suppressing insurrection or rebellion, shall not be questioned. But neither the United States nor any State shall assume or pay any debt or obligation incurred in aid of insurrection or rebellion against the United States; but all such debts, obligations and claims shall be held illegal and void. (Sec. 4, Amend. XIV)

This Constitution, and the Laws of the United States which shall be made in Pursuance thereof; and all Treaties made, or which shall be made, under the Authority of the United States, shall be the supreme Law of the Land; and the Judges in every State shall be bound thereby, any Thing in the Constitution or Laws of any State to the Contrary notwithstanding.

The Senators and Representatives before mentioned, and the Members of the several State Legislatures, and all executive and judicial Officers, both of the United States and of the several States, shall be bound by Oath or Affirmation, to support this Constitution <u>and ethical behavior</u>; but no religious Test shall ever be required as a Qualification to any Office or public Trust under the United States.

## ARTICLE. VII  RATIFICATION

The Ratification of the Conventions of three-fourths of the States, shall be sufficient for the Establishment of this Constitution between the States so ratifying the Same.

Done in Convention by Consent of the States ----

Note:  This concludes the basic straw horse (revised) Constitution.  Two additional and controversial paragraphs are suggested in Chapter 5.

# CHAPTER FIVE:     THE SOLUTION OF SIZE

In Chapter 4 the topics most favored "by the people" were discussed and added to the suggested changes in the Constitution, while in Chapter 6 the most common items favored by the elites or intellectuals will be considered.  In this chapter attention is given to additional or repeated subjects believed to be of special interest using the extended list of Appendix 4 (Jim's List).

I claim not to be a reincarnated James Madison or James Wilson but what would be the point in writing a book without a few of my own opinions.  We do know that over half  (29 of 55) of the original Convention Founders were veterans and that several of them held high positions in the military during the Revolutionary War.  For example, Madison was in the Orange County militia and Alexander Hamilton was General Washington's aide.  I'm suggesting from this that retired military officers may have some logical inputs to a constitution.  Besides being in the military, your author did write a money section for Abe's Indignation League in 1999 that is still apropos today.

> **Money and Banking:** One nagging problem which has been around since the Civil War is the use of paper money, instead of coin, and the question if such paper must be backed by some tangible asset, such as gold. There is no truly legal way to resolve this problem short of constitutional change.
>
> While fixing the money problem, delegates to a convention should review and consider what banking constraints are logical and necessary for the constitution. Don't forget the bail out (your money) of the savings and loan industry. And why are banks now getting into the securities business?
>
> Is the time correct to insist-on, and force, a balanced budget? No, it's worse than that, not only must the budget be balanced, but also the gargantuan public debt, near five trillion dollars that must be paid down to a reasonable level as a percentage of population or of GDP.

Otherwise, the U.S. dollar, backed by no tangible asset, will one day collapse, and the depression of 1929 will look like a cakewalk. Mr. Keynes, the economics guru who supported government debt in bad times also supported creating a government "surplus" in good times. We ignore his advice and our own common sense at our peril.

To spend the coming generations into a common poorhouse is not only unethical, but should be unconstitutional and illegal.[35]

So much for tooting my own early warning horn, the principle conclusion is that a modern constitution requires a section on economics since the world of finance, trade, transportation, and business-in-general has changed dramatically from the rural society of the late 18th century and most of the 19th century (see Appendix 1). And even though it is desirable to keep the constitution structure straightforward, easy to read and use, the morals and ethics of our nation have declined to the point where more rules and laws are necessary. In particular, the ethics and morality problem is true for our leaders (and athletes) who set the example for the rest of us. Further, we should put ideas in the constitution that lawyers and congressmen are not likely to put in on their own volition because such inclusion would undermine and reduce their power.

The main and principle problem as I see it is "SIZE." Not only the size of government but also the size of corporations, unions and other associations. On a second tier, the size of agencies, commissions, regulators, committees and lobbyists need reduction as well. Reducing size in general solves a myriad of problems. For example, reducing the size of the total federal government is followed by a reduction in agencies and regulators, and reducing the size of corporations automatically changes the size of unions and other anti-business organizations to some degree. As we know from recent history, too-big-to-fail (TBTF) seems to apply to governments (Greece, California) as well as it does to corporations (banks, auto-industry, etc.).

---

[35] Schmitendorf, James A., www.abesindignationleague.org, 1999.

For the government we can limit the size by constitutional law (the people's rules) as was partially done in Chapter 4 by limits for the budget and deficit. A further limit in size of government can be accomplished by restricting the numbers of employees as a percentage of population.

For corporations, law can also control the size. Capital complications will need addressing however. In both cases there is a risk of reducing the efficiency, and more so with corporations since they depend on "the invisible hand" for efficiency and restructuring. Nevertheless, both institutions are approaching out of control status and some measure of control is essential if modern society is to survive, as we know it, without deteriorating into socialism or revolutionary tyranny.

To limit the government, I will stick by my suggestions in Chapter 4 for a strictly enforced balanced budget and deficit limits. For Federal employees, I recommend a number of eight tenths of one percent of the working population (approximately 2.5 million as of 2008), including appointees and civil service. This does not include Government-Sponsored Enterprises (GSEs), since there shouldn't be any, or the military that must be a function of national security threats. The military requires war waging power (personnel and equipment) with at least 25% more war waging power than the size of all the perceived, well-studied, and documented possible enemies, just in case of a surprise attack using WMD. Since defense is 'the' primary function of the federal government, the military portion of the federal budget must always be greater than social programs, which should be relegated to the States for all activities, save perhaps those concerning Native Americans with which we have pseudo valid treaties.[36]

---

[36] There is a good deal of evidence that Native American reservations, and the associated social welfare programs, are grossly inefficient, actually do more harm than good, and should be phased out.

Let us now consider the subject of corporations. Large efficient corporations are good. Giant bureaucratic, too-big-to-fail, corporations are bad. Just as we conservatives would like to limit the size and power of government we must do the same for very large corporations. It is incongruous and irrational for us to be anti big government but not anti Goliath size businesses. The proper goal is to optimize the efficient use of both assets and labor.

There will be some variations with industry types, since certain corporations are more capital sensitive (mining, manufacturing) while others are more labor sensitive (real estate, finance, insurance). In either case there is a maximum to the number of people we would like to see out of work, as a rational society, should a giant corporation go belly-up. The size limit needs to be indexed to either the population or the GDP and with a balance between the people number and the efficiency variable. Definitely, we do not want the bureaucrats or Congress fiddling with the numbers, so they should be permanently fixed or indexed somehow in the basic Constitutional law.

A common argument against size limits is that efficiency may be decreased. I have made a rough attempt to assess corporate efficiencies using Internal Revenue Service (IRS) data from 2006 (see Appendix 5). This data was collected before the credit crisis of 2007 and therefore are perhaps a little more normal than other volatile business years. Looking at the Appendix, some of the observations are:

- For all the sectors except construction and real estate, category 12 (large corporations) dominates.

- The highest return on assets (ROA) is not in category (Cat) 12.

- The two highest ROAs are in mining (Cat 3) and in finance (Cat 2) and are generally in these categories for many other corporate sectors.

- The three lowest ROAs are in the higher categories as 0.01 for holding companies and 0.02 for finance and real estate.

- The better use of salaried personnel occurs in construction (a little surprising) and holding companies (Cat 4), not surprising.

- Low efficiencies in the use of salaried personnel are:

  information (Cat 3); finance (Cat 3); and real estate (Cat 3).

For all categories the best ROA is in mining and construction, with holding companies being the worse. Construction has the most efficient salaried personnel. Finance companies have the most assets, the highest income, and pay the most taxes, while manufacturing employs the most salaried wage earners. Note that, unfortunately, direct labor is included in the cost of goods sold and is not broken out in the IRS data.

The main conclusion is that the giant corporations are not all that efficient in the use of their assets as seen by looking across the category row for the highest ROAs, and neither does the best salary efficiency lie in the highest category. Therefore, allowing mega-corporations to dominate and not enforcing antitrust laws is operating to the detriment of us all. So what about antitrust?


Citizens can place part of the blame for TBTF at the feet of antitrust law, the lack thereof, or the lack of enforcement. Generally speaking, the U.S. government is not enforcing antitrust laws and regulations, but it is actually encouraging the mergers and acquisitions, which are helping to further concentrate industries and banking. The relationship between antitrust law and the 2008 banking /economic meltdown needs addressing.

A partial summary of antitrust law is given in Appendix 6. The basic laws are: 1) the Sherman Antitrust Act of 1890; 2) the Federal Trade Commission Act of September 1914; and 3) The Clayton Antitrust Act of October 1914. The Sherman Act passed with only one dissenting vote in Congress and gave an early indication that American did not want large dominating corporations, and the laws of 1914 amplified and supported this early pronouncement.

Although things went fairly well at times, with Teddy Roosevelt (a pro antitrust Republican) breaking up the eastern railroads in 1902-04, with the breakup of Standard Oil in 1911 under President Taft (also an antitrust Republican), and with the creation of Baby Bells from the near monopoly of AT&T in communications as late as June of 1982. However, the courts waffled several times on antitrust enforcement, just as they have with other laws.

For example, in 1948 the Supreme Court denied the United States' action against United States Steel Corporation in the acquisition of the Consolidated Steel Corporation as not an unreasonable "restraint of trade" even though U.S. Steel had an ongoing blatant record of buying up over 180 competing firms. In the five to four decision, Justice Douglas (dissenting) gave a good summary of the ills of giant corporations quoting the *Curse of Bigness* essay written earlier by Justice Brandeis.[37]

Slipping backwards with the Telecommunications Act of 1996 (see Appendix 3), the remaining portion of mother AT&T began to be eaten by its young. The Baby Bells and their offshoots made numerous mergers and acquisitions the end result being just a few

---

[37] See www.stolafedu/people/becker/antitrust/summaries/334us495.html; (retr. 6/5/2010)

98

very large corporations dominating the telecom business "again," and with one previous Baby Bell renaming itself AT&T.

The biggest snafu perhaps came when Microsoft was let off the hook. Microsoft, with an obvious near monopoly in the computer operating system software business, was challenged by the U.S. Department of Justice and 19 States in 1998 for tying product sales together, a practice clearly prohibited by the Clayton Act. After several years of shady litigation and stalling by Microsoft, the federal government backed off and the near monopoly continues to this day (4 July 2010).

The lack of regulatory and law enforcement problems increased in the 70s and continued into the 80s and 90s as it became popular to be pro laissez-faire and anti-antitrust. As the big banks and pseudo banks (e.g., AIG, Fanny, Freddie) became bigger and bigger, meltdown of the financial system was inevitable. Among the dead wrong experts on this economic disaster were prominent bureaucrats, economists, bankers, journalists and judges. For example, Henry Paulson, Milton Friedman, Richard Fuld Jr., Thomas Sowell, Robert Bork and many others just did not see the storm coming or ignored it. Why did they get it so wrong? Four reasons I believe:

1) A prime factor was an over dependence on the ethical and moral conduct of the business community. The "invisible hand" assumes a reasonable level of honesty. The named smart people above probably remember the 1950s and 1960s when we use to leave our cars and houses unlocked? Times have changed!

2) A second reason was leadership. When the big boss of the Federal Reserve (Alan Greenspan) is against antitrust--what bureaucrat supervisor will be enthused about enforcement of the laws and regulations already on the books?

3) Third, giant corporate size creates its own brand of bureaucrats that manage poorly and sometimes completely fail, just like they do in large government.

4) Finally, there is little fear of punishment. Besides Michael Milken, Bernie Madoff and a few Enron executives, our modern robber barons, are not in jail. The top five executives of all the bailed-out too-big-to-fail corporations should probably be in jail for fraudulently using derivative activities to bilk individual and institutional investors. Were it not for the lack of reasonable campaign finance laws, the higher executives probably would be in jail. That is, the politicians are protecting them. On the government side, supervisors seldom get fired because of overly protective civil service rules. Executives in government or GSEs running the Federal Reserve, Treasury Department, Office of the Comptroller, Federal Deposit Insurance Corporation, Securities Exchange Commission, Fanny Mae, Freddie Mac, etc., continue on unabated as do Congressmen (like Barney Frank) who screw up royally on their committee assignments but still have ample campaign (lobby) funds to get reelected time and time again. Indirectly stealing from the taxpayer is just as bad, and maybe even worse, than cheating the investor. Certainly, here is another very good reason for term limits.

Now let us turn to federal government organizations and regulations. A few examples of problems and failures are in order:

1.) The Antitrust Division of the Department of Justice (ADDOJ) has overlapping authorities with the Federal Trade Commission causing unnecessary duplication and a coordination nightmare. One or the other should be phased out. For example, does the FTC really need consumer games on their website, and does ADDOJ need such extensive coordination with the European Union?

2.) The pre-merger notification required by the Hart-Scott-Rodino Act (See Appendix 6) did not help since little or nothing was done to stop major mergers. Only token divestitures were imposed. This smells of political intervention. Mergers nearly doubled from 1990 to 1995 and only one percent was of concern according to the FDIC.[38] Regulators allowed more than 2600 mergers between 1991 and 2008.[39] Might that not be a clue to a problem?

3.) The federal government is trying to justify allowing banks to merger claiming larger banks are more efficient and serve the mid sized market better. Yet the regulators fail to convincingly show how they calculated bank efficiency. Should not banks just grow with the commercial market naturally?

4.) When a bank fails, the FDIC does its best to get another bank to take over its assets and operations. Short-term consumer help truly hurts the consumer in the long run. The indirect acquisition makes for larger banking corporations and trends toward oligopoly, the very thing antitrust tries to avoid.

5.) A serious occurrence of federal government unintended consequences were the incorporation of supposedly helpful regulations. The SEC mandated the use of Nationally Recognized Statistical Ratings Organizations (NRSROs). Without doubt, these financial ratings corporations (Moody's, Standard & Poor's, and Fitch) were a significant factor in TBTF because of their inept corporate ratings and management.

6.) Now comes the new 2000 plus page financial system improvement law some two years after the 2008 crash. So far (July 2010) we know the new bill does not include a solution for Fanny and Freddie and increases the number and cost of regulators. The ability to avoid TBTF remains largely unanswered, as are the details of the regulations. Both tend to slow economic development. Congress passes a law, then civil servants write the regulations. Isn't that backwards? Shouldn't the regulations be written, and then included in the law? Some positive inclusions in the new law are better transparency and derivative control. Congressional leadership on the bill by Senator Christopher Dodd and Representative Barney Frank does

---

[38] Robinson, Constance K., Director of Operations, Antitrust Div. DOJ, "Bank Mergers-Antitrust trends," before Bar Assoc. NY City, 30 Sept 1996.
[39] www.fpif.org/articles/big_oils_last_stand; (Retr. 16 Mar 2010)

not bode well however, and the unknown consequences remain to be seen. During the Senate debate only one Senator to my knowledge spoke the magic words, "these banks are too big period" and that was Senator Ted Kaufman of Delaware.

In closing this section on antitrust I would again like to point out that the Democrats want big government and tight business control, while the Republicans prefer small government and tend to tolerate big to huge businesses. I submit that the middle conservative road is both small government and small to mid-sized efficient businesses. Some relative big corporations may be necessary for capital reasons, but seldom can we justify, on an efficiency basis, super giant corporations or holding companies any more than we can justify overly large government.

Beyond antitrust, who should we blame for the 2008 financial crisis? Many tend to blame the Federal Reserve or the big banks as the culprits. I prefer Congress as the main problem. After all, they created the Federal Reserve and have oversight over the regulators. They passed the two principle Acts that caused much of the monetary disruption. Namely, the Gramm-Leach-Bliley Act of 1999, which repealed the Glass-Steagall Act of 1933, and let banks own financial firms. Then the Congress passed the Commodity Futures Modernization Act in 2000 allowing certain commodities to trade off-the-exchange with minimum oversight. Basically, these two Acts, pushed by Senator Phil Gramm, loosened the rules sufficiently to cause the crash. As with intelligence prior to the 9/11 terrorist attack, Congress failed miserably in their monitoring functions.

Second in line for blame are the regulators—civil servants with a personnel advancement system based mostly on longevity rather than accomplishment, with conflict of interest government unions, and a paper heavy dismissal method, there obviously are going to be problems. And how can the good regulators be protected from political influence? Creating a bigger bureaucracy like Homeland Security surely has little merit. Auditing helps, as do inspector generals if used without notice, but workable solutions remain unknown for such large government organizations? Even whistle blowing reward schemes have had minimal overall positive results. Smaller sized agencies in the future may be of some help.

In this final section recommendations will be made for corporate, union, and association size reduction. I see nothing wrong with using a maximum employee size based on population. For corporations, ten percent of the smallest State's latest census does not seem unreasonable. This would be in the order of 70,000. When Chrysler was bailed out the first time it had approximately 130,000 personnel, so the recommended number is about one half that value. To keep the power of unions and other economic associations at a reasonable level, my recommendation for these organizations is a limit to twice the corporate number or 140,000. If these numbers were approved at Constitution ratification time, organizations with a larger people-size would be required to divest or split-up within a given length of time, say three years.

Asset size is a tougher question. Economy and defense disruptions would be:
- To transportation (e.g., rail, air, trucks, ships etc.)
- To strategic defense effect on materials and manufacturing such as:
  - ♣ Mining of coal, oil, iron ore, alumna, manganese, etc.
  - ♣ Manufacturing of firearms, tanks, trucks, airplanes, ships, space vehicles, tires, and tools, plus the auto industry as a back up system.
- To the financial system.
- Brownouts associated with the electrical grid.
- Of the communications system, including the Internet.

- International relations.

Trying to keep changes easy to understand, my inclination is to use a percentage of the real GDP to limit assets in two ways, one for the corporations requiring large capital equipment and another for those companies without such requirements. My recommendations for asset limits are as follows:

- For mining and manufacturing (except during declared war), and for commercial banking, one percent of GDP.
- For all others, one-half this amount or one-half of one percent of the GDP.
- Alien corporations doing business in the U.S. may not exceed these limitations.

Exxon Mobil's assets in 2008 were over $ 200 billion[40] or about 1.7 % of a $12 trillion GDP. JPMorgan Chase[41] had over $ 2 trillion in assets the same year but the quality of the assets is unknown. These recommendations require that most giant corporations down size or spin-off part of their operations and would probably make a few CEOs and investors unhappy to say the least. But their implementation will improve asset efficiency, increase competition, and reduce moral hazard (TBTF). Although the effect on ROE may not be positive immediately on implementation, the efficient use of manpower and assets should improve the bottom line.

The changes in this chapter are best placed in section six of our present Constitution as revised in Chapter 4 and the following language is recommended:

ADD TO ARTICLE VI in Chapter 4, Part 3 these two paragraphs:

Paragraph Four: *Total employee or member numbers (including contracted personnel) for any corporation, union, association, or other organization involved in economic activities of any kind, may not exceed 10% of the smallest States'*

---

[40] http://money.cnn.com/magazines/fortune/global 500/2009/snapshots/387.html: Retrieved 10 March 2010.
[41] www.google.com/finance?q=JPM; Retrieved 10 March 2010.

*population. Nor may such groups with similar avocations collude in leadership or monetary support. Political parties and religions are exempted from this requirement.*

Paragraph Five: *Corporations of mining, manufacturing and commercial banking must limit their assets (leases included) to no greater than one percent of the average last five years of positive real GDP. All other corporations or organizations are limited to assets of one-half of this amount.*

To close this chapter, let us remember the importance and greatness of capitalism. From the FTC Guide to the Antitrust Laws: "Free and open markets are the foundation of a vibrant economy. Aggressive competition among sellers in an open marketplace gives consumers—both individuals and businesses—the benefits of lower prices, higher quality products and services, more choices, and greater innovation."[42]

Ayn Rand, the heroine of capitalism, would not have agreed with my antitrust analysis. But in this rare instance Ayn, Alan Greenspan, Michael Medved and others are in error for completely distrusting the government's concern with big business operations. The financial meltdown of 2007-2008 seems to prove the point, and an example of 2010 would be the problem with British Petroleum and the Gulf of Mexico oil well explosion and leak. In some cases the Government just has to be trusted, or fixed so it can be trusted, in the realm of giant corporations, just like it is for the military in national defense.

---

[42] www.ftc.gov/bc/antitrust/index.shtm; (Retr.1 June 2010)

## CHAPTER SIX        PROPOSALS OF THE ELITE

Assume for a moment a convention has been called by the Congress or the States, then what are the most common proposals that would or should be considered by the intellectual community?  There is a large variety to choose from.  The author's notes contain over 300 ideas in Appendix 4. Surprisingly, when one reviews *Vile's*[43] book with 40 plus contributors, you obtain a similar number of over 300 subjects.  Many of these proposals can be handled by Congress as extra-constitutional solutions, if only Congress would act, or by the political parties.  Others are more structural in nature and conducive to constitutional change.

The goal of this book continues to be a constitution that "constrains" the Executive, Congress and the Judiciary from arbitrary interpretations of the Constitution.
The task of this chapter is to choose the best proposals from *Vile's* book, which would accomplish the most without cluttering up the Constitution with excess verbiage.

I will discuss primarily the subjects from *Vile* with multiple occurrences (hits) by over ten percent of the authors, organizations, commissions etc.  The list below gives the approximate percentage of the total number of times a topic is mentioned.  For example, if 20 of the 40 authors mention a particular subject, the percentage is 50 percent.

## SUBJECTS FROM *VILE* WITH 10 PERCENT OR MORE HITS:

| | | |
|---|---|---|
| 1. Convention | 38% | |
| 2. Parliamentary System | 31% | |
| 3. Presidential Power | 30% | |
| 4. Congress/Executive Togetherness | 27% | |
| 5. Electoral System | 26% | |
| 6. Treaties | 22% | |
| 7. Extended Terms | 22% | |
| 8. Cabinet Legislators | 22% | |
| 9. Judicial Power | 18% | |
| 10. Voting Rights | 18% | |

---

[43] John R. Vile, *Rewriting the U.S. Constitution,* (Praeger Publishers, 1991).

| 11. Amendment Methods | 18% |
| 12. Party Conventions | 17% |
| 13. Legislative Regions | 16% |
| 14. Budget/Debt | 15% |
| 15. No Vice President | 15% |
| 16. Corporation Control | 15% |
| 17. National Referendum | 13% |
| 18. Revolution Possible | 13% |
| 19. Line Item Veto | 13% |
| 20. Taxes | 13% |

## ITEM 1: CONVENTION
:

Note that the largest category (38%) is that we "should have a convention." Strangely, few of the authors go into any detail on how to have one. Some wanted the States to supply delegates while others preferred that Congress or the President appoint the attendees. Few authors feared a runaway convention or opening Pandora's box. This fear is overstated since ratification would be necessary. As William MacDonald explained; "we are not trying to cause a revolution, but trying to prevent one."[44] Mario Pei points out that the States update their constitutions—so why can't the Federal government?[45] For Thomas Brennan it was; "whether it is better to alter our fundamental law through a process of judicial interpretation and legislative and executive encroachment combined with popular acquiescence, or whether it is better to change the constitution..."[46] This writer endorses the use of a convention every 50 years and Chapter 7 covers the "how-to" in depth. The State governors and legislators need to show some leadership, courage and guts to get the convention initiated and functioning.

## ITEMS 2, 4 and 8: PARLIMENTS & TOGETHERNESS:

These three items go together since they are interrelated and stem from the British system. Woodrow Wilson may have been the first to suggest we switch to a parliamentary system, but he later changed his mind. There have been many other authors through the years who preferred all or part of the English method of governing. They

---

[44] Vile, p. 59.
[45] Ibid, p. 100.
[46] Ibid, p. 128.

107

liked the ideas of less secrecy, a question and answer period, and a better way to oust the leader with a no-confidence-vote that keeps the government more accountable.

More joint committees, opposite party cabinet members, combined education classes and more social activities would improve the overall attitude and effectiveness of Congress and the Executive. If congresspersons were required to actually show up at committee meetings and floor discussions it would help. A drawback to socialization is our modern transportation system that allows congressmen to return to their home State and families on weekends and holidays.

Bringing legislative members into the cabinet (Item 8) arouses critics because it subverts the chain-of-command vital to good management. It would also increase the workload on persons already unable to produce a budget on time or avoid omnibus bills.

One should point out the failure of the British parliamentary system to stem World War II when their government (according to C-SPAN documentaries) had ample chances to dispose of Hitler in the late 1930s. Sticking to our checks and balances may not be particularly efficient and granted, the accountability is weak; nevertheless, the English system works reasonably well because of their long history of common law and their unwritten constitution, while parliamentary methods in other nations have not been so fortunate.

Only a minor change in the Constitution would be necessary to allow legislators to be cabinet officers, but they shouldn't get double pay, and the workload addition seems unreasonable. The President could easily have a question and answer period on alternate months with the House and the Senate. Executive officers could sit on congressional committees to answer questions. The Congress and Executive officers might arrange more social activities together. Most of these "togetherness" items don't require change in the structure of our Constitution. Parliamentary items such as no-confidence votes would necessitate a modification.

## ITEM 3; PRESIDENTIAL POWER:

If you reduce the power of the President too much you run the risk of not having strong leadership in an emergency situation. This usually does not become a major problem because both the Congress and the people acquiesce and seed necessary power in emergencies to the President as they did in World War I, II and after 9/11. Nevertheless, a minor consensus of the elites seems to be that the President has too much power, worrying he might become a pseudo King or despot, and that the impeachment method is far too weak.

The reduction of war powers was covered in Chapter 4. The increase in House terms in Chapter 4 would indirectly "increase" Presidential power. Item 18, the line item veto, would also increase his power if included in the Constitution. So more needs to be done to offset these effects if Presidential power is to be reduced.

There are at least three areas remaining which could be changed to lessen the President's power: (1) judicial and officer appointments, (2) executive orders, and (3) pardons and reprieves. It's impossible to run the Executive Department without being able to give an order, but executive orders are a form of legislation and should at least be time limited. The other two areas, appointments and pardons, could be reduced partially or altogether. For example, a first no-confidence vote in Congress could reduce or discontinue his pardon and reprieve power, a second no-confidence vote could decrease his appointment powers, and a third might call for removal and a new election. A sort of three strikes and you're out scheme. Another variable could be the level of no confidence. Should it be 3/5, 2/3, 3/4, 4/5 or unanimous, or should the level change with each succeeding vote? This is workable, but complicated, and violates the secondary goal of keeping the constitution fairly basic and straightforward. A better solution is to transfer judiciary appointment directly to senior State judiciaries, pardon/reprieve power to the federal judiciary, and leave officer appointments to the President. A clear definition of "misdemeanors" is also essential to improve impeachment power. The judicial subjects receive further attention in item nine below.

## ITEM 5; ELECTORAL SYSTEM:

Elimination of the Electoral College in favor of a popular election is a recommendation of several elites. The system is a little undemocratic and could easily be removed from the Constitution. But does it really hurt anything? I agree here with Sabato[47] and the Founders that there might be an outside chance of fraud or the public could be ill informed. In these cases the electors serve as a safe guard of sorts. The College also preserves a degree of power for small States much like the Senate. Therefore, this change is not recommended.

## ITEM 6; EXTENDED TERMS:

The elites not only want the House terms extended to four years as the people do in Chapter 4, but the Senate to eight years as well. Some also wanted to extend the President's term, or to do so if he were voted "in-confidence" by the legislature. These changes, except for the House, are unnecessary in my estimation since the drawbacks of long extended terms and repeated terms has corruption and old age factors well supported by history.

## ITEM 7; TREATIES:

It is illogical to have the State and Defense Departments, along with the Executive, to work years negotiating a treaty and then have the Senate disapprove it. The saddest example is the League of Nations disapproval that might have deferred World War II, had our Senate not rejected it. Former long term Senator J. William Fulbright complained about our divided government making agreement with foreign governments as "tentative and provisional."[48]

The concurrence of both houses by majority vote recommended by several of *Vile's* authors is probably too lenient. A better judgment would be approval by a 3/5 vote of the whole Congress (now 2/3 in the Senate alone). This would decrease Senate power and increase House (the people's) power.

---

[47] Sabato, p 138.
[48] Vile, p. 150.

## ITEM 9; JUDICIAL POWER:

From *Vile*, Walter Clark[49] was irate about five men being able to nullify the Congress. He wanted the Supreme Court to be elected with fixed terms and subject to popular recall and Congressional override. Another and more serious problem started after World War II with the Supreme Court beginning to make their own law—the so-called judicial activism. Several books, magazine and newspaper articles have covered this subject. Two fairly recent books: Judge Andrew P. Napolitano's *Constitutional Chaos*[50] and Mark R. Levin's[51] *Men in Black* support the conservative elite side of this topic in detail.

The elite's basic problem with judicial power began with *Marbury v. Madison* when the Supreme Court established "for themselves" the right to declare laws unconstitutional thereby usurping the power of the Congress. (See examples in Appendix 2 and 3.) The power of the people lying primarily with the House, it seems reasonable that they might have the final say in such cases by a high percentage vote, after reviewing the language of a rejected bill. (See Appendix 7 for Judiciary and Supreme Court basics.)

On the other hand, if we the people are going to let *Marbury v. Madison* stand, then the Constitution needs to be changed to make the Supreme Court's power legitimate and historically viable. This would be the author's choice; otherwise we would have a major mess with previous Supreme Court cases. Still, some of the Court's functioning edicts could be overthrown. For example, mid or late term abortions.

## ITEM 10; VOTING RIGHTS:

Item ten is not about "one person one vote" which came from a case about redistricting; rather, it is about literacy in voting. Several of *Vile's* authors were concerned with voters voting without reasonable knowledge about what they are voting

---

[49] Ibid, p. 52
[50] Andrew P. Napolitano, *Constitutional Chaos,* (Nelson Current, 2004), 157, 194
[51] Mark R. Levin, *Men in Black*, (Regnery Publishing, 2005), 14, 23-29

for. Sean Hannity's "man on the street" Fox TV program also pretty well illustrates the point. We have citizens voting, even though supposedly literate, who don't have a clue about how a republic works—a major slap in the face of our liberal education system.

Connecticut adopted the first literacy test in 1855, but the Supreme Court later outlawed it in *Guinn v. United States* in 1915, citing the 15th Amendment. In *Vile,* Ralph Cram[52] disliked universal suffrage and William MacDonald[53] was in favor of voter qualifications.

Most democrats prefer that every person be able to vote regardless of their knowledge about an election, in order to obtain or preserve their political power. Opposite of the concern of early American Colonists, one could make a reasonable argument about "no representation without taxation." That is, non-taxpayers voting to subsidize themselves are a direct conflict of interest.

It is not likely at this stage in democratic government that we will take away from adults the right to vote (except felons). One possible solution would be to use weighting factors based on education or position. For example; the basic taxpayer would get one vote; a high school graduate, 1.25 votes; a college grad or entrepreneur 1.5 votes, etc.

## ITEM 11; AMENDMENT METHOD:

The amendment methods are too strict and difficult according to the elites and they propose a variety of changes. More State involvement and recurring conventions were two ideas. One author in *Viles's* book, Alexander Hehmeyer,[54] proposed a convention every 30 years; similar to the idea of Thomas Jefferson's comment about generations making their own laws. The "people's rules" certainly need review in every couple of generations, but even every hundred years would be more reasonable than our current condition. For sure, the Congress is not very good at amendments and the suggestion that the States control the process makes a lot of sense.

---

[52] Vile, p. 76
[53] Ibid, p. 58
[54] Ibid, p. 91

## ITEM 12; PARTY CONVENTIONS:

Party problem solutions have no business in the Constitution in my opinion. Not that they don't exist and need fixing, but the scope of the Constitution cannot include or solve all of the people's difficulties in organizing their own associations and procedures. Donald L Robinson's book *Reforming American Government, The Bicentennial Papers of the Committee on the Constitutional System* has several articles about the party system. The Founders ignored factions hoping we would all be independents—not a bad idea.

## ITEM 13; REGIONS:

Constitution changing authors had concerns about Congress members being too State orientated at the detriment of the various regions of the nation. Some authors even went so far as to recommend doing away with States altogether in lieu of regional areas to take their place. Regions varied from five to fourteen in number. This is a drastic change basically forbidden by the Constitution without approval of the affected States and the Congress. Regional Senators from groups of States was another suggestion. There does appear to be a lack of national representation in the Congress as opposed to State representation.

## ITEM 14; BUDGET AND DEBT:

This subject was addressed in Chapter 4 and will not be discussed further here. The only detail given by any of *Vile's* authors was a limit on military spending. Others wanted to limit the debt and have a specific budget but gave no explicit suggestions.

## ITEM 15; NO VICE PRESIDENT:

Although the Vice President normally doesn't have much of a job, he has replaced the President on occasion. In addition, only the President and Vice President are elected by all the people. Rather than getting rid of the position it would be better just to give him a job, such as Secretary of State.

## ITEM 16; CORPORATE CONTROL:

All the intellectual socialists want strict corporate control or in the extreme case, such as William K. Wallace, actual government ownership of major industries.[55] President Truman tried to control the steel industry during the Korean War but was refuted by the Supreme Court in the Steel Seizure Case of 1952.[56] Ironically, *Vile's* elites give little support to capitalism and entrepreneurship, the things that make the United States strong and wealthy.

It appears that the administration and the 111th Congress have been able to control and partially take ownership of banks and car companies during the recession of 2008, 2009, and 2010, without Supreme Court disapproval. There is nothing in the present Constitution that allows Congress or the President such takeovers. However, during major wars, such as the Civil War and World War II, the practice was common.

## ITEM 17; NATIONIAL REFERENDUM:

With the advent of the extensive Internet the possibility of moving the "peoples' rules" closer to a pure democracy is within sight. For instance, voters could be given a voting password at voter registration and the password used to electronically vote on serious government questions such as impeachment, war, etc. Persons without computers could use the public libraries for their input.

## ITEM 18; REVOLUTION:

By and large, the conservatives prefer a revolution of words and votes to cure our government ills. But several of the elite authors in *Vile's* book believe the problem is more serious and a physical revolution may be possible, or even necessary, to improve our condition.

The tyranny of excessive government control over our lives is possible to the point where violence may be necessary, and it becomes closer every year as more socialism

---

[55] Vile, p. 68

[56] *Youngstown Steel & Tube Co. v. Sawyer*, 343 U.S. 579 (1952).

occurs. If you are thinking along these lines you should read the history of the French Revolution. Physical revolutions can turn really nasty with unintended consequences and really worse tyranny. Tea Parties and voter education are better.

The dire predictions of *Vile's* authors were made mostly after the Great Depression and Henry Hazlitt worried during World War II that we might loose the war without Constitution improvements.[57] James Sandquist's prediction of economic collapse nearly came true in 2008 and 2009.[58] Let us hope that Tea Parties are not the precursor to more violent assemblies. It would be better if the Constitution were improved before violence occurs.

## ITEM 19; LINE ITEM VETO:

A line item veto for the President was suggested after the Civil War,[59] again after the Great Depression in 1935 by William Y. Elliott,[60] and still later by Malcolm Eiselin in 1937.[61] I see nothing wrong with this elite recommendation as long as the legislation override remains in place. It would be clumsy for omnibus legislation but omnibus legislation is not good legislation in the first place, for it just indicates the Congress is slow and incompetent in getting their work accomplished.

The line item veto would also put a stop to some pork barrel legislation. It works at the State level. It could reduce debate on bills, speed up legislation, and make the pocket veto less likely.

On the negative side is the argument that a line item veto would transfer some legislative (purse) power to the Executive. In addition it provides a bargaining item that could further corrupt the governing process and increase Presidential power as mentioned in item three. In 1995 a Line Item Veto Act was passed by the Congress but later declared

---

[57] Vile, p. 85.
[58] Ibid. p. 131.
[59] Sandquist, p. 281.
[60] Vile, p. 73
[61] Ibid, p. 75

115

unconstitutional by the Supreme Court in 1998, as a violation of the Presentment Clause.[62] (See Appendix 2)

## ITEM 20; TAXES:

Jeremy M. Miller was in favor of a maximum and minimum tax rate.[63] Implied with item fourteen and the budget problem would be reduced spending, but except for Mr. Miller none of *Vile's* authors were specific about tax limitations. Neither were elites vocal about increasing taxes to support their social programs. No one talked about double taxation, corporate taxes or taxes on investments.

## ADDITIONAL ITEMS:

Since management books often indicate that the majority or higher consensus solutions to problems are not always the best, I should mention a few elite topics that I believe are good ones, but are only mentioned by one or two authors.

For example: 1. Establish an academy for civil servants similar to the military
academies. (By Ralph Cram)[64]

2. At-large national Senators. (By William Y. Elliott)[65]

3. Five States may challenge a Supreme Court ruling.
(By Council of State Governments)[66]

## CONCLUSION:

In this chapter I have attempted to consolidate and summarize the desires of the elites. Some of these subjects coincide with those of "the people" in Chapter 4 such as House terms and budget limits. The elites gave the topics of campaign-finance and ethics little attention, although these two topics were mentioned by a few (less than 10%) of *Vile's* authors. None of the elite proposals have been reduced to Constitutional language

---

[62] Heritage Guide to the Constitution, p. 88.
[63] Vile, p. 147.
[64] Ibid, p. 77.
[65] Ibid, p. 73.
[66] Ibid, p. 98-99.

in this chapter since the theme for this book is closer to a middle class and blue-collar peoples' approach.

A convention would probably consider many of the elite proposals and additional types of suggestions. (See Appendix 4)  The next and final chapter will cover ideas for an unbiased convention.   This is of particular importance for persons who contend that a convention might result in drastic liberal type changes in the Constitution to our detriment.

# CHAPTER SEVEN    PERIODIC REVISIONS by CONVENTION

One of the biggest fears of changing the Constitution is that one faction or another will gain control of the convention and make changes to their advantage. This chapter is a plan to resolve such a fear. The method is to update the Constitution periodically by having a convention and to choose the participants "by lot" using the following rules:

Qualifications:
1. Natural born citizen age 40 to 75
2. Physical condition—excellent (must pass a second class FAA physical and a missile launch officer psychoanalysis test).
3. Education—advanced degree from an accredited university, more than one bachelor's degree, or an IQ (Wechsler Scale) over 120.
4. Restrictions—no felons, multiple misdemeanors, or previous federal office holders.
5. Pass a general college level civics examination on the Constitution and Constitutional law.
6. Experience— business owner, manager, supervisor, non-fiction author, teacher, scientist, farmer/rancher, engineer, military officer or master sergeant, journalist, etc.

Application Agreement:
1. To being sequestered for three months (mid June to mid September)
2. To study (read) the Federalist and Anti-Federalist papers as well as at least five other books about the U.S. Constitution prior to the convention.
3. To not discuss convention activities with outside agencies during the convention. (No leaks)
4. To choose the professional area that is the best fit for their experience in one of the five categories listed below.

Preliminary Selection:
By lot, with State legislatures as witnesses, the governor of each State selects ten names from each of five professions to be in the final drawing. If applicants for a profession are less than ten in number, all the applicants will be eligible. The process is to be monitored by each State Secretary of State and a federal Marshal.

Final Selection:
By lot, and witnessed by each State legislative body, the governor of each State shall be blindfolded and draw one final delegate and one alternate from a tumbled box with a hand-sized opening containing the preliminary remaining applicants. If a State has a population from the previous federal mandated census exceeding 10% of the total national population census, such as California, New York or Texas, then a second set of delegates will be drawn for convention attendance for that State.

Administration:   The five largest States in population shall provide administrative support with five staff library members, plus one alternate, and all must volunteer to the three month sequester.  The second five largest States will provide security and each State shall fund its delegate(s) to the convention at a remote mountain resort and pay participants twice their normal House pay rate plus travel expenses.  The convention shall choose its own leadership and determine its schedule.

Results:   The convention majority approved results in a form similar to the present Constitution will be placed on the Internet and printed by contract bid with State funding (according to population) and distributed to the media and each taxpayer at least one month prior to the next general election cycle.  Extra copies will be made available at cost.

Approval:   In the general election the people will either approve or disapprove the revised Constitution by a majority vote.  If approved it must then be confirmed by a vote of at least three-fourths of the Sate legislatures for ratification.  Given confirmation, it will stand for the next 50 years or other agreed to period and amended by whatever amendment procedure is included in the document.  If disapproved the process will be repeated before the next general election.

List of Professions:  Academic, Scientist or Engineer, Business Manager, Entrepreneur or Self-Employed, State or Local Politician.

(Note that lawyers who do not fit in one of these categories are not eligible, nor are federal judges or federal politicians because of their conflict of interest)

---

Other schemes or methods for a convention that would eliminate or minimize the bias of lawmakers are certainly possible.  One would be to assign the project to the military and see what they come up with.  Their mid-grade officers are generally nonpartisan because they are under oath to serve the President and his administration regardless of which party is in power. Colonels and generals however become more political. The committee method used in *The Bicentennial Papers* mentioned in Chapter 1 did not seem very constructive.

Whatever method might be used to update the Constitution, it would be more functional and easier to read if the language was revised within the document as amendments are adopted. This is a fairly common practice in aircraft documents wherein revised pages are published for insertion into a loose-leaf manual as new information becomes available and then periodically a new section or the whole document is republished. These documents, often called Technical Orders, contain the very important operating instructions and maintenance directives revised regularly for safety reasons. There is no good reason the Constitution could not be handled in a similar manner to incorporate amendments as adopted. In addition, given the importance of the document, it's probably a good idea to number each paragraph or even each line.

## CONCLUSION

As of July 2010 the latest Gallup poll for Congress approval stood at eleven percent. Perhaps the lowest ever! When the power elite politicians, supported by the modern lobbyists, continue to spend the wealth of unborn generations, one begins to understand the Jacobins and demand that something be done.

The above Convention method leaves negligible possibility for faction bias. The professional categories tend to balance variations in ideology. Strict constructionists and fearful conservatives must begin to believe the numerous polls (e.g., Pew in June 2010) that show the public favoring the right (39%) and the middle (36%), considerably more than the left (22%).

Appendix 4 provides plenty of fodder for consideration but there is no need to completely open Pandora's Box. The convention can be limited in scope, or number of subjects, just as done in Chapters 3, 4 and 5. The primary idea is to limit considerations to topics the Congress refuses to fix, along with obvious modernizations. In any case, the changes must be approved by ratification.

Nearly every pundit panel agrees the system is broken. The people must petition their State Governors and their State legislators for a convention to revise the Constitution and the Governors must "lead" in order to regain State power and to set the United States on a path for another two hundred years of excellence. This is the answer.

# EPILOGUE

From a reproduction of Justice Joseph Story's Book: *Commentaries On The Constitution of the United States*, (Brown, Shattuck, and Co., 1833), Chapter XLI, § 956-959

"Upon this subject little need be said to persuade us, at once, of its utility and importance. It is obvious, that no human government can ever be perfect; and that it is impossible to foresee, or guard against all the exigencies, which may, in different ages, require different adaptations and modifications of powers to suit the various necessities of the people. A government, forever changing and changeable, is, indeed, in a state bordering upon anarchy and confusion. A government, which, in its own organization, provides no means of change, but assumes to be fixed and unalterable, must, after a while, become wholly unsuited to the circumstances of the nation; and it will either degenerate into a despotism, or by the pressure of its inequalities bring on a revolution. It is wise, therefore, in every government, and especially in a republic, to provide means for altering, and improving the fabric of government, as time and experience, or the new phases of human affairs, may render proper, in order to promote the happiness and safety of the people. The great principle to be sought is to make the changes practicable, but not too easy; to secure due deliberation, and caution; and to follow experience, rather than to open a way for experiments, suggested by mere speculation or theory.

In regard to the constitution of the United States, it is confessedly a new experiment in the history of nations. Its framers were not bold or rash enough to believe, or to pronounce it to be perfect. They made use of the best lights, which they possessed, to form and adjust its parts, and mould its materials. But they knew, that time might develop many defects in its arrangements, and many deficiencies in its powers. They desired, that it might be open to improvement; and under the guidance of the sober judgment and enlightened skill of the country, to be perpetually approaching nearer and nearer to perfection. It was obvious, too, that the means of amendment might avert, or at least have a tendency to avert the most serious perils, to which confederated republics are liable, and by which all of them have hitherto been shipwrecked. They knew, that the besetting sin of republics is a restlessness of temperament, and a spirit of discontent at slight evils. They knew the pride and jealousy of state power in confederacies; and they wished to disarm them of their potency, by providing a safe means to break the force, if not wholly to ward off the blows, which would, from time to time, under the garb of patriotism, or a love of the people, be aimed at the constitution. They believed, that the power of amendment was, if one may so say, the safety valve to let off all temporary effervescences and excitements; and the real effective instrument to control and adjust the movements of the machinery, when out of order or in danger of self-destruction.

Upon the propriety of the power, in some form, there will probably be little controversy. The only question is, whether it is so arranged, as to accomplish its objects in the safest mode; safest for the stability of the government; and safest for the rights and liberties of the people.

Two modes are pointed out, the one at the instance of the government itself, through the instrumentality of congress; the other, at the instance of the states, through the instrumentality of a convention ...."

# APPENDIX ONE:  CULTURE COMPARISON

| LATE 18TH CENTURY (1700s) | EARLY 21ST CENTURY (2000s) |
|---|---|
| Household:<br>Outhouses, trenches, shallow wells, creek water, cisterns, tubs, washboards | Household:<br>Toilets, showers, running water, deep wells, spas, hot tubs, washing machines |
| Transportation:<br>Land:  Horses, oxen, mules.<br>     Stage coaches, Conestoga wagons,<br>     gigs, buggies, carts, sleds,<br>     Roads:  dirt, macadam gravel, stone<br><br>Water:  Row boats, sailing boats/ships,<br>     schooners, canoes, ferries, barges,<br><br><br>Air:  Balloon<br>     (1st balloon flight Amer. 1793) | Transportation:<br>Land:  Cars:  gas, diesel, hybrid, electric<br>     Trucks:  pickups, utility, semi's<br>     Trains: diesel/elect, bullet. Bicycles<br>     Roads:  paved, freeways<br><br>Water: Row, speed, sailing boats<br>     Utility (diesel/gas) barges, tugs, etc.<br>     Ships (steam, diesel, nuclear), yachts,<br><br>Air/Space:  Planes; single/multiengine<br>     land and sea, (gas, jet)<br>     Balloons, gliders<br>     Space ships, satellites |
| Medical:<br>Country doctors, bleeding, leaches, hand made false teeth, crude hospitals | Medical:<br>Specialty doctors, pain/miracle drugs, antibiotics, organ transplants, X-rays, MRIs, CAT scans, mega hospitals |
| Food/Agriculture:<br>Fireplace cooking/ovens, Dutch ovens, barrel commodities, grist mills, ice houses, vegetables and fruits in season, farm markets, dried/salted meat, hardtack, hand/horse plows, hand harvest, | Food/Agriculture:<br>Microwave/gas/electric ovens, frozen/canned foods, fresh vegetables/fruits/meat year around, boxed cereals, dehydrated/organic foods, supermarkets, refrigeration, large diesel/gas tractors, wheeled/powered harvest/field equipment. |
| Weaponry:<br>Flintlock muskets, smooth bore cannon, knives, swords, bow and arrows, catapults, rams, mortars, torpedo-mines.<br><br><br>Ships of the line, frigates, cutters, sloops of war, galleys, barges | Weaponry:<br>Rifles, machine guns, bazookas, mortars, flamethrowers, mines, torpedoes<br>Rifled cannon, field guns, tanks<br>Fighters, bombers, helicopters<br>Cruisers, destroyers, aircraft carriers, patrol boats, mine sweepers, amphibious assault ships, hover/landing craft, submarines<br>Missiles—short, medium, intercontinental<br>Bombs--atomic, hydrogen, biological, chemical, fragmentation, smart, bunker busting |

TIMES HAVE CHANGED AND SO SHOULD THE CONSTITUTION

# APPENDIX 1, PART 2:  SELECTED INVENTIONS SINCE 1787
### (How Engineers and Scientists Have Changed Our Nation)

| | |
|---|---|
| Adhesive Tape | 1923-1930 |
| Air Brake System | 1869 |
| Airplane | 1903 |
| AC Circuit Transmission | 1888 |
| Air Conditioning | 1906 |
| Air Bags | 1973 |
| Aluminum Modern Process | 1980s |
| Anesthesia | 1846-1939 |
| Aspirin | 1900 |
| Assembly Line | 1901-1913 |
| Atomic Reactor | 1955 |
| Auto Glass Developed | 1904 |
| Auto Transmission | 1911 |
| Automatic Lubrication | 1872 |
| Ballpoint Pen | 1935 |
| Band Aid | 1920 |
| Barbed Wire | 1874 |
| Barcodes | 1948 |
| Barometer | 1843 |
| Bicycle (improved) | 1866 |
| Bottle Cap | 1892 |
| Bread Slicer | 1927 |
| Calculating Machine | 1888 |
| Caller ID | 1984 |
| Camera (roll firm) | 1888 |
| Cash Register | 1879 |
| Cellular Phones | 1960-1980s |
| Color Film | 1936 |
| Computer | 1945-1954 |
| Computer Compiler | 1952 |
| Contact Disposable Lens | 1995 |
| Cotton Gin | 1794 |
| Crayons | 1903 |
| Cyclotron | 1934 |
| CT Scan | 1975 |
| Debit Cards | 1995 |
| Diesel Engine | 1898 |
| Digital Cameras | 1986 |
| Disposable Diaper | 1950 |
| Dry cell Batteries | 1870 |
| DVDs | 1995 |

| | |
|---|---|
| Magnetic Tape Recorder | 1900 |
| Maser | 1958 |
| Mechanical Pencil | 1942 |
| McCormick Reaper | 1834 |
| Microphone | 1880 |
| Microwave Oven | 1946-1954 |
| Motion Pictures (silent) | 1893 |
| Motorcycle | 1867 |
| Magnetic Resonance Imaging | 1977 |
| Navigation Localizer | 1954 |
| Navigation Omnidirectional | 1950s |
| Nylon | 1937 |
| On-line Stock Trading | 1994 |
| Oral Contraceptive | 1954 |
| Organ Transplants | 1967 |
| Pad Lock | 1848 |
| Paper Clip | 1899 |
| Pasteurization | 1873 |
| Phonograph | 1878 |
| Photography | 1829-1879 |
| Plastics (Bakelite) | 1907 |
| Plough (cast iron) | 1797 |
| Polaroid Camera | 1937 |
| Polio Vaccine | 1947 |
| Potato Chips | 1853 |
| Power Point | 1987 |
| Printing Press (rotary) | 1847 |
| Q-Tips | 1920s |
| Radar | 1935 |
| Radar (Doppler) | 1990 |
| Radio (code) | 1895 |
| Radio (wireless) | 1914 |
| Radioactive Isotopes | 1940 |
| Rayon | 1855-1924 |
| Road Reflector | 1933 |
| Record Player | 1877 |
| Reel (manual) Lawnmower | 1830 |
| Revolving Gun | 1836 |
| Rocket (liquid fueled) | 1907-1919 |
| Rubber Band | 1845 |
| Safety Pin | 1849 |

| | | | |
|---|---|---|---|
| Dynamite | 1867 | Safety Matches | 1855 |
| E-Mail | 1999 | Satellites | 1958 |
| Electric Dishwasher | 1960s | Satellite TV | 1994 |
| Electric Iron | 1882 | Sea Plane | 1922 |
| Electric Refrigerator | 1803-1915 | Sewing Machine | 1846-1861 |
| Electric Starter | 1903 | Smoke Alarm | 1976 |
| Electric Streetcar | 1835 | Space Craft | 1957 |
| Electric Welder | 1886 | Spray Can | 1927 |
| Electron Microscope | 1931 | Steamboat | 1812 |
| Electronic Tolls | 1989 | Steel (Bessemer) Process | 1850s |
| Elevator Brake | 1854 | Stereo Audio Systems | 1950s |
| Escalator | 1891 | Storage Batteries | 1859 |
| Fertilizer (artificial) | 1859 | Telephone | 1876 |
| FM (frequency modulation) | 1933 | Television | 1930 |
| Frozen Food | 1930 | Television (flat-panel) | 1960s |
| Gas Mask | 1914 | Tin Can | 1810 |
| Genetic Engineering | 1973 | Toilet Paper | 1857 |
| Gyroscope | 1852 | Tractor/Gasoline | 1892 |
| Helicopter | 1932 | Tractor/Steam | 1868 |
| iPods | 2001 | Transformer | 1891 |
| Induction Motor | 1900 | Transistor | 1950 |
| Insecticide (DDT) | 1943 | Triode Vacuum Tube | 1907 |
| Integrated Circuit | 1959 | Tungsten Filament | 1913 |
| Internal Combustion Engine | 1877 | Typewriter | 1867 |
| Internet | 1969 | Umbrella | 1852 |
| Jet Engine | 1946 | Vacuum Cleaner | 1899 |
| Kevlar | 1971 | Velcro | 1948 |
| Laptop Computers | 1983 | Video Tape Recorder | 1958 |
| Laser | 1960 | Vulcanized Rubber | 1844 |
| Laser Printer | 1975 | Washing Machine | 1900 |
| Light bulb (long lasting) | 1879 | Windshield Wiper | 1903-1905 |
| Light Emitting Diodes | 1970 | World Wide Web | 1990 |
| Linotype | 1884 | Wrench (adjustable) | 1922 |
| Lithium Batteries | 1991 | Xerography | 1938 |
| Loom (powered) | 1837 | X-Ray | 1895 |
| Magnetic Core Memory | 1955 | Zipper | 1893-1923 |

IT SHOULD BE OBVIOUS FROM THIS APPENDIX THAT OUR SOCIETY HAS CHANGED SIGNIFICANTLY WHILE OUR CONSTITUTION REMAINS BASICALLY TIED TO THE EIGHTEENTH CENTURY.

# APPENDIX TWO:   CONSTITUTION CLAUSE LIST AND BRIEFS

## SELECTED ITEMS FROM THE CONSTITUTION AND AMENDMENTS
THIS IS A PARTIAL, BUT EXTENSIVE, ALPABETICAL INDEX WITH
MINI BRIEFS ON STARED (*) CONTROVERSIAL ITEMS

## CLAUSE LIST

1.  Admiralty_____        Art. III, Sec. 2, Cl. 1 (Const. Ratified June 1788)
2.  Appointment
    a. Senate _____Art. II, Sec. 2, Cl. 2
    b. Recess _____Art. II, Sec. 2, Cl. 3
3.  Appropriation _____ Art. I, Sec. 9, Cl. 7
4.  *Arms, Keep & Bear _____Amend. II (Amend. I thru X ratified Dec. 1791)
5.  Arraignment _____ Amend. VI
6.  Borrowing _____ Art. I, Sec. 8. Cl. 2
7.  *Citizenship _____ Amend. XIV (Rat. 9 July 1868)
8.  *Coinage _____ Art. I, Sec. 8, Cl. 5
9.  *Commerce _____ Art. I, Sec. 8, Cl. 3
10. Compensation_____    Art. I, Sec. 6, Cl. 1
11. Confrontation_____ Amend. VI
12. *Contracts _____Art. I, Sec. 10, Cl. 1
13. *Counsel, Right To _____ Amend. VI
14. Cruel and Unusual _____Amend. VIII
15. *Diversity _____ Art. III, Sec 2, Cl. 1
16. *Double Jeopardy _____ Amend. V
17. Due Process
    a. *Federal _____ Amend. V
    b. *Civil War _____Amend. XIV
18. *Equal Protection _____ Amend. XIV, Sec. 1
19. Enforcement _____Amend. XIV, Sec. 5
20. Enumeration _____ Art. I, Sec. 2, Cl. 3
21. *Establishment, Religion _____Amend. I
22. Expulsion _____ Art. I, Sec. 5, Cl. 2
23. *Free Speech/Press _____Amend. I
24. Grand Jury, Exception _____ Amend. V
25. Impeachment
    a. President _____ Art. I, Sec. 5, Cl. 2
    b. Standards _____ Art. II, Sec. 4
26. Incompatibility_____ Art. I, Sec. 6, Cl. 2
27. Judicial, Appellants _____ Art. III, Sec. 2, Cl. 2
28. *Jury, Civil Cases _____ Amend. VII
29. *Jury Trial_____ Amend. VI
30. *Lame Duck _____ Amend. XX (Rat. Jan. 1933)
31. *Necessary and Proper _____ Art. I, Sec. 8, Cl. 18
32. Oaths _____ Art. VI, Cl. 3

Clause List Continued

33. Origination _____ Art. I, Sec. 7, Cl. 1
34. Pardon _____ Art. II, Sec. 2, Cl. 1
35. Presentment
    a. Bills to President _____ Art. I, Sec. 7, Cl. 2
    b. Resolution _____ Art. I, Sec. 7, Cl. 3
36. *Privileges and Immunities _____ Amend. XIV
37. Reexamination _____ Amend. VII
38. *Reserved Power to States _____ Amend. X
39. *Rights Retained by People ____Amend. IX
40. *Search and Seizures _____ Amend. IV
41. Self Incrimination _____ Amend. V
42. Senate Elections _____ Amend. XVII (Rat. Apr. 1913)
43. *Speedy Trial _____Amend. VI
44. Spending _____ Art. I, Sec. 8, Cl. 1
45. Suffrage
    a. Race, Color, Servitude_____ Amend. XV (Rat. Feb. 1870)
    b. Sex _____ Amend. XIX (Rat. Aug. 1920)
    c. Age 18+ _____ Amend. XXVI (Rat. July 1971)
46. *Supremacy _____ Art VI, Cl. 2
47. *Take Care _____ Art. II, Sec. 3
48. *Takings _____ Amend. V
49. Taxes
    a. Direct _____ Art. I, Sec. 9, Cl. 4
    b. Income _____ Amend. XVI (Rat. Feb. 1913)
    c. Poll _____ Amend. XXIV (Rat. Jan. 1964)
50. Treason _____ Art. III, Sec. 3, Cl. 1
51. *Treaty _____ Art. II, Sec. 2. Cl. 2
52. Vesting
    a. Legislature _____ Art. I, Sec.1
    b. *President _____Art. II, Sec. 1, Cl. 1
    c. *Judicial _____ Art. III, Sec. 1
53. Veto
    a. Legislative _____ Art. I, Sec. 7, Cl. 2
    b. Line Item _____ Art. I, Sec. 7. Cl. 2
    c. Pocket _____ Art. I, Sec. 7. Cl. 2
54. Warrant _____ Amend. IV
55. *Welfare, General _____Preamble and Art. I, Sec. 8
56. Witness _____ Amend. VI

Notes: The basic Constitution was completed in September 1787 and ratified by the necessary nine States in June of 1788. The first ten Amendments were ratified in December 1791. The ratification dates of other Amendments are indicated on the list.

# MINI BRIEFS ON CONTROVERSIAL CLAUSES
{Numbers refer to the list above}

4. Keep and Bear Arms (Amend. II): A recent Supreme Court decision (*District of Columbia v. Heller*, 2008) confirmed the individual right to possess firearms without any connection to a militia.

7. Citizenship (Amend. XIV): Persons born or naturalized in the U.S. and subject to U.S. jurisdiction are citizens. A main purpose of the Amendment was to give the slaves citizenship. The Fourteenth Amendment also reversed the *Dred Scott* case. The 39th Congress did not explain details of the 14th Amendment as the Founders did for the main Constitution using the Federalist and Anti-Federalist papers.

8. Coinage (Art. I, Sec. 8, Cl. 5): Violated in *Veazie Bank v. Fenno*, 75 U.S. 533 (1869), using the Necessary and Proper Clause. Later *Legal-Tender* cases further supported issuance of paper money by the federal government.

9. Commerce (Art. I, Sec. 8, Cl. 3): This Clause rivals both the First and Fourteenth Amendments in the number of Supreme Court cases. The Court gave Congress complete and extensive commerce powers in *Gibbon v. Ogden*, 22 U.S. 1 (1824). Eventually the Clause was used to cover just about every aspect of business short of items manufactured and sold in a single State, and went so far as to regulate activities which might at some future date affect interstate commerce. As usual, the Court waffled somewhat depending on its internal makeup. The Court attempted to partially standardize their rulings with *Pike v. Bruce Church Inc.*, 397 U.S. 137 (1970).

12. Contracts (Art. I, Sec. 10, Cl. 1): Contract obligations were important to the Founders. Early decisions by the Court (*Dartmouth College, 1819 and Charles River Bridge, 1837)* stuck to the contract wording. Later, by the New Deal era, Courts allowed exceptions like mortgages and social interest items, thereby reducing contract and rule of law enforcement.

13. Counsel, Right To (Amend. VI): *Miranda* extended this Clause to the "presence of counsel." It has also been extended to appeals. But the Court decided petty offenses might be excepted if incarceration is not a factor. Court appointed counsel for the poor is now required.

15. Diversity (Art. III, Sec 2, Cl. 1): These Clauses were a basic mistake by the Founders because they forgot about State immunity. The First Congress corrected the mistake with the Eleventh amendment. The "between Citizens of different States" portion of the Clause didn't work much better and several statutes were required to systemize its operation.

16. Double Jeopardy (Amend. V): One cannot be tried twice for the same serious offense. It has applied to the States since 1969. Exceptions include impeachment, mistrials, some confinements, etc. The 18th Amendment violated this Amendment.

17. Due Process (Amend. V and Amend. XIV): The Clause was extended to the States through the XIV Amendment. It is a frequently used Clause which confirms legality, and that the "rule of law" be applied in an orderly fashion. At first, the 14th Amendment was used primarily to protect ex-slaves. However, the Clause has been widely abused by judicial activism and remains in frequent dispute. The New Deal was a turning point and after the 1950s the Court made several liberal and "substantive" interpretations, including: wide definitions for liberty, welfare protection, agency rule making, right of privacy, abortion rights, homosexuality, etc. Using "life, liberty, or property" the Clause can be used to include most any interest or loss thereof. In an early case (*Lochner v. New York, 1905*) the Clause was used to strike down a law limiting work hours. By 1965 (*Griswold v. Connecticut*) it was used in the contraceptive case to invent the right to privacy.

18. Equal Protection (Amend. XIV, Sec. 1): As another major portion of the 14th Amendment, the broad scope of the Clause remains a quandary since "equality" is so difficult to define. Voting rights and social rights are not addressed in the Amendment but the Clause bolstered the support of the Civil Rights Act of 1866. *Plessy v. Ferguson* (1896) introduced the concept of "separate but equal." *Brown v. Board of Education* overturned this ruling in 1954. More recently the worm of discrimination has begun to crawl into the equal protection equation. So now the Court must decide what scrutiny to give other classifications such as sex, same-sex, age, disability, women, races besides African-Americans, etc. The Court now applies the Clause to local governments as well as State and Federal.

21. Establishment, Religion (Amend. I): Congress cannot establish a national religion. However, there is no doubt that the Founders supported Christian religion for its importance in increasing virtue and morality, the necessary ingredients for good government. The Court has made a variety of decisions on the subject in need of some standardization.

23. Free Speech/Press (Amend. I): This Clause still produces lots of lawyer fees. For example, libel laws make sense while sedition laws did not fly. There is a morality problem with pornography and "yelling fire" in a theater while the Courts extension to expressive views like flag burning and money-equals-speech upsets lots of citizens. *Buckley v. Valeo* (1976) is a good example of the speech versus money difficulty.

28. Jury, Civil Cases (Amend. VII): The twenty-dollar rule has long been out-of-date but never revised by additional Amendment. Both the legislature and the Courts have basically ignored the civil case jury requirement and have made up their own rules.

29. Jury Trial (Amend. VI): For some cases the Court has changed the number of jurors from twelve to six, and also has started to allow less than unanimous votes for conviction. In addition, the Court has begun to hear felony trials without juries, using plea-bargaining instead. The complications of the modern courtroom, sentencing guidelines, and budget limitations have negated the trial-by-jury right as originally intended.

30. Lame-Duck (Amend. XX): The President's and Congress's term beginning dates were originally established by the Confederation Congress in the spring (4 March) to avoid winter travel and allow elector information time to get to the Capitol. Given the election dates established by most States in late Fall (early November), a lame-duck (do-nothing period) between election and taking office resulted. To make matters worse, the first day of Congress operation didn't start until early December (Art. I, Sec. 4). Thus there could be 13 months between election and participation. The Founders basically goofed in organizing the Congressional calendar and it's amazing the problem was not fixed until 1933. This Amendment reduced the dead period to about two months but did not completely solve the problem. Other parts of the 20th Amendment concern administration and Presidential succession.

31. Necessary and Proper (Art. I, sec.8. Cl. 18): Supposedly restricted to subjects covered in the Constitution, the Clause has been grossly confused and abused by the Court to cover almost any subject. *M'Culloch v. Maryland* (1819) attempted to moderate use of the Clause but by using the Commerce Clause the "stretch" has been widespread to support several laws and Amendments. On the other hand, the Constitution could not function well without this Clause or something similar. For example, the Clause is needed to affect the other enumerated powers of Congress and general organization of the government. The Marshall Court, as consistent with the Clause, therefore approved the Bank of the United States requested by Alexander Hamilton.

36. Privileges and Immunities (Amen. XIV, Sec. 1): This Clause is similar to Article IV, Section 2, Clause 1, but as part of the 14th Amendment applies within the States as well as between States. Its purpose was to stop the "Black Codes" of the Southern States and enforce the Civil Rights Act of 1866 that included such items as buying, selling, contracting, travel, security, property rights, etc., within all States. However, as with other Clauses, the meaning and substantive interpretation varied with several different Supreme Courts. Only after multiple

cases over decades was segregation beginning to be truly solved with *Brown v. Board of Education.*

38. Reserved Power to the States (Amend. X): As with Amendment IX, the Court violates this Amendment with regularity. The Court seldom limits the Congress to its enumerated powers allowing the federal government to meddle in such areas as regulating State employment policies and withholding funds when States rebel.

39. Rights Retained by People (Amend. IX): This Amendment contradicts the Necessary and Proper Clause of Article II and the case *M'Culloch v. Maryland (1819)* fairly well made the Amendment null and void.

40. Search and Seizures (Amend. IV): Applicable to most arrests, this Clause causes a prolific number of lawsuits. It spawned both the "reasonableness rules" and the "exclusionary rule" used in several cases such as *Weeks v. U.S. (1914)* and *Mapp v. Ohio (1961).*

43. Speedy Trial (Amend. VI): Required for criminal cases, this cause is grossly violated by the Courts on a regular basis.

46. Supremacy (Art. VI, Cl. 2): Federal laws trump State laws but Treaties do not trump the Constitution.

47. Take Care (Art. II, Sec. 3): This Clause is somewhat repetitive of the President's Vesting Clause, but still adds confusion about the power of independent agencies in the execution of laws. The refusal to enforce laws or to use appropriations was reputed in *Youngstown Sheet & Tube Co. v. Sawyer (1952).*

48. Takings (Amend. V): Both natural law and common law protect property. Government eminent domain power with reasonable compensation also uses the Necessary and Proper Clause. The Court has upheld a city's right to take property for other than direct public use, an abomination. There appears to be no set of mathematical rules and the effects of near-by takings remains a continuing problem.

51. Treaties (Art. II, Sec. 2, Cl. 2): The Senate has abrogated its advice portion of the Clause and lets the Executive branch negotiate and write treaties. The Senate's two-thirds approval requirement has on occasion raised Constitutional questions such as treaty termination and Executive "Agreements" which remain unresolved.

52b. Vesting, President (Art. II, Sec. 1, Cl. 1): The President is vested in the executive power to enforce laws and perform foreign affairs (along with the Senate) except for items exclusively reserved to the Congress such as declarations of war and commerce regulation. The President's administrative power was confirmed in *Myers v. U.S. (1926)*; however *Morrison v. Olson (1988)* supports independent councils and limits executive privilege.

52c. Vesting, Judicial (Art. III, Sec. 1):  This Clause establishes a separate and independent judiciary to interpret the law, use the facts, and decide binding judgments.  With the Judiciary Act of 1789 Congress established upper level inferior courts with mostly lifetime terms under good behavior and with no salary reduction possible.  A lower (Article II) category of Judges may be executive employees.  The Supreme Court gave to themselves additional power and decided on their own to control what law would be constitutional in *Marbury v. Madison (1803)* and established their power over State law and regulations in *McCulloch v. Maryland (1819)* and *Lochner v. New York (1905)*.  After the New Deal, the Court began to take on and decide social issues.

55. The General Welfare (Preamble and Art. I, Sec. 8, Cl. 1) clause, according to most of the Founders, was intended for the nation as a whole and not for local or State benefit.  The clause has been grossly abused by the legislature and usually without Supreme Court objection.

Author's Note:  It should be clear from the above paragraphs that the Supreme Court is at least partially broken, that they are occasionally making decisions based on their own ideology, and not using strict interpretation of the Constitution as written.  Revision of the open ended Clauses (e.g., 9, 17, 31, 55) of the Constitution and more standardization would be very helpful. Further information on the Supreme Court is given in Appendices 3 and 7.

# APPENDIX THREE:  CONGRESSIONAL ACTS OF INTEREST

This appendix is broken down in three sections and gives a selected list followed by a mini explanation of a few Acts.  Topics do not include "social" Acts because the author believes social welfare, including education, should be left to the States and not included in the Federal Constitution. Agriculture Acts are numerous and vary widely with the weather and the economy, so are not included. Transportation laws included (well beyond post roads) are limited to railroad Acts. Tax bills vacillate with the economy as the legislature attempts to control fiscal policy. Stared (*) items on the list have short briefs at the end of the section.  These items are either historically important or include some judicial ramification. To give the reader a feel for Supreme Court interpretations, some overruled items are explained. A secondary code (#) indicates that a new federal government agency or commission was created by the Act.  Duplications exist for bills with more than one common name.  Neither the list nor the briefs are intended to be all-inclusive.

The three topic areas are:

Section I:   Budget, Economics & Taxes
Section II:  Defense & Military
Section III: Voting & Campaign Finance

## Appendix 3, Section I, Part 1:  BUDGET, ECONOMICS & TAXES

1. Adamson Act, 1916
2. Airline Bailout, 2001
3. Airline Deregulation, 1978
4. American Recovery & Investment Act, 2009
5. *American Stamp Tax, 1898
6. *Anti-trust (Sherman) Act, 1890
7. Balanced Budget and Emergency Deficit Control Act, 1985
8. Banking (Emergency) Act, 1933
9. *Banking Reform Act (Gramm-Leach-Bliley), 1999
10. Bituminous Coal Conservation Act, 1935
11. Budget Conciliation Act, 1987
12. Budget Deal, 1996
13. Budget (Omnibus) Reconciliation Act (Gramm-Latta II), 1981
14. Cable Communications Policy Act, 1984
15. Cable TV Regulations Act, 1992
16. Child Labor Tax Act, 1919
17. Chrysler Bailout, 1979
18. Communications Act, 1934
19. Community Reinvestment Act, 1977
20. *Commodity Futures Modernization Act, 2000

21. Congressional Budget & Improvement Control Act, 1974
22. Consumer Credit Protection Act, 1968
23. Consumer Product Safety Act, 1972 (#)
24. *Corporate Responsibility (Sarbanes-Oxley), 2002
25. Credit Card Accountability, Responsibility Disclosure Act, 2009
26. Curb on Shareholder Lawsuits, 1995
27. Curb on Un-funded Mandates, 1995
28. Deal to Balance Budget by '02, 1997
29. Deficit Reduction Measure, 1984,1987
30. Deficit Reduction Package, 1990
31. Deficit (Omnibus) Reduction Act, 1993
32. Depository Institutions & Monetary Control Act, 1980
33. *Dodd-Frank Wall Street Reform & Consumer Protection Act, 2010
34. Economics Act, 1933
35. Economic Recovery Tax Act, 1981
36. Economic Stabilization Act, 1970
37. *Economic (Emergency) Stabilization Act (TARP), 2008
38. Economic Stimulus Package, 2008
39. Embargo Act, 1807
40. Employee Retirement Income Security Act (ERISA), 1974
41. Energy Bill, 1975, 2007
42. Equal Credit Opportunity Act, 1974
43. *Estate Tax Law, 1919
44. Fair Housing Act, 1968
45. Fast Track Trade Authority, 2002
46. Federal Food, Drug & Cosmetic Act, 1938
47. Federal Reserve Act, 1913
48. Federal Trade Commission Act, 1935 (#)
49. Financial Services Modernization Act, 1999
50. Foreign Insurance Tax Act, 1954
51. Fraud Enforcement & Recovery Act, 2009
52. Full Employment & Balanced Growth Act, 1978
53. General Agreement on Tariffs & Trade (GATT), 1994 (#)
54. Glass-Steagall Act, 1933
55. *Gramm-Leach-Bliley Act (see 9 & 42 above), 1999
56. Gramm-Rudman-Hollings Anti-Deficit Act, 1985
57. Garn-St Germain Depository Institutions Act, 1982
58. Harbor Maintenance Tax, 1986
59. Hawley-Smoot Tariff Bill, 1930
60. Health Maintenance Organization Aid Act, 1973
61. Hiring Incentives to Restore Employment Act, 2010
62. Home Owner's Loan Act, 1934
63. *Income Tax Act, 1916
64. Internal Revenue Service Overhaul, 1998
65. Interstate Commerce Act, 1887
66. Judicial Improvements Act, 1990

67. Landrum-Griffin Labor Reform Act, 1959
68. *Legal Tender Acts, 1862-63
69. Loan (Emergency) Guarantee Act, 1971
70. National Banking Act, 1964-5
71. National Gas Act, 1938
72. National Industrial Act, 1934
73. *National Industrial Recovery Act, 1933
74. North American Free Trade Agreement, 1993
75. Omnibus Government Spending, 2009
76. Rail Passenger Service Act, 1971 (#)
77. Railroad Bankruptcy Reorganization Amendment, 1980
78. Railroad Retirement Act, 1934
79. Reconstruction Act, 1867
80. Regional Rail Reorganization Act, 1973
81. Revenue Act, 1962
82. Revised Bailout Bill, 2008
83. *Safety Appliance Act, 1893
84. *Sarbanes-Oxley Act (see 24 above), 2002
85. Savings & Loan Bailout, 1986 & 1989
86. Securities Act Amendment, 1975
87. Securities Exchange Act, 1934 (#)
88. Securities Litigation Reform Act, 1995
89. *Sherman Antitrust Act (see 6 above), 1890
90. Social Security Act, 1935 (#)
91. Taft-Hartley Act, 1947
92. Tariff Act, 1894
93. Tax Cut, 1977, 2003
94. Tax Cut (Bush), 2001
95. Tax Cut (Kennedy), 1964
96. Tax Law Overhaul, 1954
97. Tax Reduction, 1971, 1975
98. Tax Reform Act, 1969, 1976, 1978, 1982
99. Tax Reform & Rate Reduction (Reagan), 1986
100. Telecommunications Reform Act, 1996
101. Trade & Tariff Act, 1984
102. Trans-Alaskan Pipeline, 1973
103. *Troubled Asset Relief Program (TARP), 2008 (see 37 above)
104. Trucking Deregulation, 1980
105. Truth in Lending, 1968
106. Volstead Act, 1920
107. Wagner Act, 1935
108. Worker, Home-Ownership & Business Assistance Act, 2009

———————————————

Appendix 3, Section I, Part 2: Mini Explanations for Stared Items.

Item 5: American Stamp Tax, 1898: This tax Act on exports violates Article I, Section 9 of the Constitution. *Fairbank v. United States,* 181 U.S. 283 (1901), a 5/4 decision.

Item 6 & 89: Sherman Antitrust Act, 1890: The first antitrust law. (See Appendix 6 for this and several other antitrust Acts.)

Item 9 & 55: Banking Reform (Gramm-Leach-Bliley) Act, 1999: A major screw-up by the congressional banking committees and President William J. Clinton. The bill was passed in a lame duck December session and allowed commercial banks and investment banks to merge. It was a major cause of the late 2000's deep recession.

Item 20: Commodity Futures Modernization Act, 2000: Another major reason for the 2008 recession. President George W. Bush signed the bill that allowed off-exchange and unregulated trading of derivatives.

Item 24 & 84: Corporate Responsibility (Sarbanes-Oxley) Act, 2002: Accounting requirements overhauled as a result of the Enron Corporation scandal and regulation changes caused by the Securities Litigation Reform Act (Item 88) of 1995.

Item 33: Wall Street Reform & Consumer Protection (Dodd-Frank) Act, 2010: A basic result of the 2008 recession and banking/stock market crash. The bill's name reflects more of the problem than solution. The Fanny Mae and Freddie Mac mortgage writing and holding problems were not solved.

Item 37 & 103: Economic (Emergency) Stabilization Act (TARP), 2008: A bank bailout fund established to save the U.S. and maybe the World's banking system at the request of the Treasury Department and the Federal Reserve.

Item 43: Estate Tax Law, 1919: Partially ruled as seizure of private property in violation of the Fifth Amendment by the Supreme Court in *Nichols v. Coolidge*, (1927).

Item 63: Income tax Act, 1916: The portion about taxes on stock dividends held by the Supreme Court invalid because dividends are not a direct tax. *Eisner v. Macomber* (1920). Later allowed with multiple Congress changes in recent years.

Item 68: Legal Tender Acts, 1862 & 63: Supreme Court flip flopped on their ruling that paper money could not be used to pay debts contracted before Act passage and did require gold backup. Several "legal tender cases" were involved with the Court using Article I, 8; Article I, 10; and the Fifth Amendment. The basic Act was originally used to help fund the Civil War.

Item 73: National Industrial Recovery Act, 1933: Perhaps the most frequently referenced law of the New Deal it attempted to delegate transportation and economy rules to the executive branch. It was partially declared unconstitutional for lack of specifics. *Schechter Poultry Corp. v. United States & Panama Refining Co. v. Ryan* (1935)

Item 83: Safety Appliance Act, 1893: Applied to railroad equipment, the Act was one of the first to be upheld using the Necessary-and-Proper plus the Commerce Clause. (see Appendix 2)

## Appendix 3, Section 2, Part 1: DEFENSE & MILITARY ACTS

1. ABM Treaty, 1972
2. Aid to Pakistan, 2009
3. Alien Registration (Smith) Act, 1940
4. *Alien & Sedition Acts, 1798
5. Anti-terrorism Act, 1996
6. Arms Control and Disarmament Agency, 1961 (#)
7. Army Reorganization Act, 1916
8. Authorization of Use of Military Force, 2001
9. *Calling Forth (Uniform Military) Act, 1792
10. Chemical Weapons Convention Ratification, 1997
11. Communist Control Act, 1954
12. Comprehensive Iran Sanctions Accountability and Divestment Act, 2010
13. Conscription Act, 1863
14. Conscription Act, 1917
15. Defense Bill, 2009
16. Defense Department Reorganization, 1958
17. Defense Production Act, 1950
18. Detainee Treatment Act, 2005
19. Dick (Military) Act, 1903
20. Draft Lottery, 1967
21. Embargo Act, 1807
22. Espionage Act, 1917
23. Expatriation Act, 1868
24. Federal Aid Highway Act, 1956 (#)
25. Foreign Intelligence Surveillance Act, 1978
26. Goldwater-Nichols Reorganization Act, 1986
27. Homeland Security Department Act, 2002 (#)
28. Illegal Immigration Reform & Immigrant Responsibility, 1996
29. *Immigration and Nationality Act, 1940, 1944
30. Intelligence Authorization Act, 1991, 2004, 2005--2010
31. Intermediate Range Missile Treaty, 1988
32. Iraq Incursion Act, 2002
33. Iraq Resolution, 2002
34. Labor Management Reporting & Disclosure Act, 1959
35. Lend Lease Act, 1941
36. Marshall Plan, 1948

37. McCarran Internal Security Act, 1950
38. Mexican Fence Bill, 2006
39. Military (Dick) Act, 1903
40. Military Extraterritorial Jurisdiction Act, 2000
41. NASA Act, 1958
42. *National Defense Act, 1916
43. *National Security Act, 1947
44. National Security Agency Terrorist Monitoring Act, 2007
45. Nationality Act, 1940
46. NATO Treaty, 1949 (#)
47. NATO Expansion, 1998
48. Neutrality Act, 1935
49. Nine-Eleven Commission, 2002 (#)
50. Nuclear Nonproliferation Treaty, 1969
51. Nuclear Test Ban Treaty, 1963
52. *Oath Test, 1865
53. Outer Space Treaty, 1967
54. Panama Canal Treaty, 1978
55. Persian Gulf Resolution, 1991
56. *Posse Comitatus Act, 1878
57. Postal Services & Federal Employees Salary Act, 1962
58. Riot Act, 1786
59. Sedition Act, 1918
60. Selective Service Act, 1917, 1948
61. Selective Training & Service Act, 1940
62. Smith (Alien Registration) Act, 1940
63. Strategic Arms Reduction, 1992
64. Strategic Offensive Reduction Treaty, 2003
65. *Subversive Activities Control Act, 1950
66. Trading With The Enemy Act, 1917
67. Truman Doctrine, 1947
68. *Uniform Code of Military Justice, 1950, 1956
69. *Urgent Deficiency Appropriations Act, 1943
70. USA Patriot Act, 2001
71. Use of Force Act, 2001
72. War Labor Disputes (Smith-Connally Anti-Strike) Act, 1943
73. War Powers Act, 1973
74. Weapons System Acquisition Reform Act, 2009
75. Wearing Military Apparel, 1956

---

## Appendix 3, Section 2, Part 2: Mini Explanations for Defense (*) Items

Item 4: Alien & Sedition Act, 1798: The early Supreme Court used the Act to punish some of Jefferson's supporters indicating political Court bias from the vary beginning. The Act clearly trampled the First Amendment. History buffs frequently reference this Act.

Item 9: Calling Forth (Uniform Military) Act, 1792: Congress gave President Washington authority to call forth the militia for eminent dangerous conditions. It was used during the Whiskey Rebellion in 1794. States have concurrent authority (*Huston v. Moore, 1820*).

Item 29: Immigration and Nationality Act, 1940,1944: Supreme Court concluded (five to four) the Act deprived draft dodgers who left the country of their Fifth and Sixth Amendment rights. (*Kennedy v. Mendoza-Martinez, 1963*)

Item 42: National Defense Act, 1916: Made the National Guard part of the regular Army and under Army control.

Item 43: National Security Act, 1947: Created the Air Force and removed the Navy from Department level.

Item 52: Oath Test, 1865: An attorney, previously pardoned by the President, was refused permission to appear before a federal court because he could not give oath as to having not engaged in actions of hostility against the United States. In *Ex parte Garland* the Supreme Court decided (5/4) that this was interference with the pardon power (Art. II, Sec. 2, Cl.1) and the ex post facto law (Art I, Sec. 9, Cl. 3).

Item 56: Posse Comitatus Act, 1878: This Act prohibits use of the military to aid civil law enforcement unless ordered by the President.

Item 65: Subversive Activities Control Act, 1950: Members of communist organizations were required to register and held to have committed a crime if attempting to obtain or use a passport. Supreme Court (6/3) held this violates "due process" under the Fifth Amendment. (*Aptheker v. Secretary of State, 1964*)

Item 68: Uniform Code of Military Justice, 1950, 1956: The purpose of the Act was to standardize military practices, penalties and justice system. It also established a special court of appeals. However, the Supreme Court did some flip flopping between military and federal jurisdiction; e.g., *O'Callahan v. Parker (1969)* was reversed by *Solorio v. United States (1987)*. Terrorism ( 9/11) has added further confusion to the situation.

Item 69: Urgent Deficiency Appropriations Act, 1943: Congress attempted to exempt certain employee's pay from appropriated funds. The Court forbid the procedure using Article I, Section 9 as enactment of a bill of attainder and ex post facto. (*United States v. Lovett, 1946*)

## Appendix 3, Section 3, Part 1:  VOTING & CAMPAIGN FINANCE

1. *Administrative Procedure, 1946
2. *Bipartisan Campaign Finance Reform (McCain-Feingold) Act, 2002
3. *Civil Rights Act, 1866
4. *Communications Act, 1967
5. *Federal Corrupt Practices Act, 1911
6. *Presidential Election Campaign Fund Act, 1971
7. *Federal Election Campaign Act, 1972, 1974
8. Federal Election Campaign Act, 1976
9. Indian Civil Rights Act, 1968
10. *Line Item Veto, 1996
11. McCain-Feingold Act, 2002 (see 2 above)
12. *Reconstruction Act, 1867
13. *Voting Rights Act, 1870
14. Voting Rights Act, 1965
15. *Voting Rights Act, 1970
16. Voting Rights Extension Act, 1970

## Appendix 3, Section 3, Part 2: Mini Explanations on Stared Voting Items

Item 1:  Administrative Procedure, 1946:  Authorizes agencies to function with the power of legislation; including fines, penalties, and judicial like proceedings.

Item 2:  Bipartisan Campaign Finance Reform Act, 2002: In January 2010 the Supreme Court again flip flopped on campaign finance by reversing much of this Act using the First Amendment. Corporations, unions, etc., are now again allowed to spend as they wish on elections. *(Citizens United v. Federal Election Commission, 2010, {5/4})*

Item 3:  Civil Rights Act, 1866:  Passed prior to the 13th and 14th Amendments to give multiple rights in the Southern States regardless of color and against the Black Codes.

Item 4: Communications Act, 1967 & 1981 amendment:  Banning non-commercial stations receiving public funds from editorializing violates the First Amendment. *(FCC v. League of Women Voters, 1984, {5/4})*

Item 5:  Federal Corrupt Practices Act, 1911: Using Article I, Sec. 4 the Congress does not have the power to fix maximum Senator candidate expenditures. *(Newberry v. United States, 1921 {8/1})* Overturned by *United States v. Classic, 1941.*

Item 6: Presidential Election Campaign Fund Act, 1971:  Independent committees cannot be limited to $1,000 expenditures for a Presidential candidate accepting public funds because it violates the First Amendment right of free speech. *(FEC v. National Conservative Political Action Committee, 1985 {7/2})*

Item 7: Federal Election Campaign Act, 1972, amended 1974: Certain provisions violate the Constitution not only by limiting expenditures but also violate the appointments clause by creating a commission appointed by Congress. *(Buckley v. Valeo, 1976 {7/2})*

Item 10: Line Item Veto, 1996: Declared unconstitutional as a violation of the Presentment Clause, Art. I, Sec. 7, Cl. 2, but several other delegation type laws continue.

Item 12: Reconstruction Act, 1867: This Act forced black suffrage on the Southern States. Later enforced by XV Amendment, 1868.

Item 13: Voting Rights Act, 1870: Provisions supporting State voting qualification laws held valid under the 15th Amendment. *(United States v. Reese, 1876 {9/0})*

Item 15: Voting Rights Act, 1970 with amendments: Changing the voting age to 18 held beyond the powers of Congress. *(Oregon v. Mitchell, 1970, {5/4})* Later fixed by the XXVI Amendment.

# APPENDIX FOUR: JIM'S LIST

## TEA PARTY BULLETS FOR A CONVENTION

This collection of subjects was taken primarily from C-SPAN and various newspaper opinion pages in South Dakota and Florida from 1999 through 2004. Some near duplications may occur. Convention members need to pick out the Tea Party type items Congress will never pass. The author does not necessarily agree with all statements. As in the Constitution, the first three subject areas are:

**I Congress, II President, and III Judiciary.**

The remaining subject areas are in a semi-order of importance:

**A. Constitution, B. Law (statutory), C. Administration (executive), D. Economy, E. Taxes, F. Corporations, G. Campaign Finance, H. Education, I. Unions, J. Media, K. Voting, L. Military, and M. Miscellaneous**

(Original black bullet dots were changed to numbers for easier reference)

## I CONGRESS:
- 1. Fewer lawyers in Congress or give up the bar to serve.
- 2. Consider extra regional Senators.
- 3. No nepotism on Capitol Hill.
  4. No racial or faction caucuses.
  5. All congresspersons must be on the floor and/or in committee meetings when debate of a bill is in progress or guests are being questioned.
  6. No bill can pass without floor discussion
  7. Omnibus bills with unrelated subjects are prohibited.
  8. Earmarks (pork) are prohibited.
  9. Foreign aid should be limited to a small percentage of real GDP.
  10. Index salaries to the real GDP.
  11. Age should be limited to one year less than the statistical gender longevity.
  12. Special education of at least 100 hours required for new legislators. (e.g., on operations, rules, and ethics)
  13. No foreign negotiations by an independent congressperson or group of congressmen or other influential citizens unless approved by the State Department.
  14. Senators may not place excessive "holds" on executive appointees and must use a time limit for an up-or-down vote.

15. We have a Vice President, why not Vice Senators or Vice Representatives? For example, someone left at home, easy to contact and alive, in case of a Washington DC disaster.
16. If the filibuster rule is so important, why isn't it in the Constitution?
17. Congressperson overseas travel is limited to two trips per year and will not be used to try to influence foreign affairs without executive approval. Violation punishment is removal without pension. (see 13 above)
18. Should super-rich people be allowed to use large amounts of their person wealth for campaigning to become a Congressman?
19. Congresspersons must be removed from committees that make serious mistakes. (e.g., 9/11 intelligence, 2008 finance)
20. Repeal the franking privilege; it favors the incumbent.
21. Retired Congressmen or their immediate relatives may not be lobbyists.
22. No electioneering on the floor.
23. Maximum of five absences from committee or floor discussions. (Violation: forfeiture of one month's pay with a public reprimand letter sent to the associated press of the State represented)
24. Announcements of federal government project approvals may not be made by incumbents prior to release to the associated press. (i.e., favors incumbent)
25. Former congressmen may not accept foreign emoluments within five years of departing the government.
26. No congressional retirement may exceed 50% of their salary.
27. No spouses, or blood relatives, or step family members of congressmen may be lobbyists.
28. Congresspersons may not insult or excessively grill persons at committee meetings.
29. Congress may not give away taxpayer money or make blanket grants without appropriation detail, but may back low interest small business loans.
30. Congresspersons should have federal, state, corporate or military experience.
31. Congress must prioritize their work to defense, intelligence, and foreign affairs and not give preference to social programs.
32. Congressmen may not vote on bills for which they have a conflict of interest.
33. Incumbents may not use government facilities or transport for campaigning.
34. Legislators may not change parties between elections.
35. Congresspersons may not roam in and out of meetings causing duplications of questions and answers, repetition of which wastes time and money.
36. Candidates for congressional office must post their résumés and their current issue-position essay at post offices, courthouses, and local newspapers and on a suitable web page at least two months prior to elections.
37. Congress must not neglect their oversight duties.
38. Failures of Congress must have repercussions. (see 23 above)

39. The federal government should cease and desist all social programs within five years or transfer them to the States.
40. Congress has had over 200 years to solve their corruption, dishonesty and ethics problem. This needs a strict solution.
41. Senators are often not present on Mondays and Fridays. (see 23 above)
42. Congress will not pass better anti-trust laws because they get many of their campaign contributions from large and giant corporations.
43. Congresspersons may not run for President and keep their Senate or House seat.
44. Committees are too large and numerous. (e.g., there are four CIA oversight committees with 70 congressmen)
45. Congressional leaders may not place special considerations in new legislation in order to get a congresspersons vote. (i.e., bribery using taxpayer funds)
46. An enumerated powers Act is needed so laws can be traced to the Constitution.
47. Post offices and large bridges should be named for soldiers killed in action, not politicians.
48. The Internet could be used to recall congresspersons.
49. Each congressman's staff must include at least one military officer and one economics/budget/accounting expert.
50. No congressperson gets a private airplane.
51. Congressional ground vehicles provided by the government shall be no newer than the oldest airplane flown by the armed services.
52. Congress may not nationalize or establish and maintain any commercial business of any type except in time of declared war.
53. Witness tables in committee hearings should be at equal height to those of congresspersons. (i.e., no talking down to citizens)
54. Books must be kept using the accrual method.
55. Sentences in government documents should have a word limit.
56. The Department of Housing and Urban Development is too prone to corruption and should be closed down.


## II PRESIDENT AND VP:

57. Reduce, eliminate, or have the Judiciary approve pardons. Pardons set the President above the law and decrease the importance of the rule of law and the appeals system. No pardon power after impeachment.
58. Time limit executive orders.
59. Index salaries to the real GDP.
60. Limit taxpayer support of Presidential libraries.
61. Former Presidents will not be pseudo foreign ambassadors.
62. The Senate "must" convict impeached Presidents if they have broken a statutory law or violated the Constitution.
63. Former Presidents may not accept payment for appearances in foreign countries within five years of leaving office.
64. Eliminate former Presidents' office expense.

65. A White House overnight stay may not be used as a pay-off for campaign contributions.
66. Judge appointment is a hold over from monarch days and is a disruption to legislation.
67. No recess appointments.
68. The President may not give favors to congressmen for votes.
69. The use of "signing statements" to avoid vetoing laws that have sections which violate the Constitution is forbidden.
70. Presidential candidates must have a pre-run security clearance and physical.
71. There must be no conflict of interest for financial appointees.
72. When commercial polls have the President below 40% approval there should be an Internet referendum to determine if a new election is required.
73. The VP needs an additional "real" job such as Secretary of State or Treasury.
74. The VP does not get a private airplane.

## III  JUDICIARY  (Also see Appendix 7)

75. If the Supreme Court has waffled or changed their position on a specific subject, the Constitution obviously needs attention or correction. (see Appendix 2 & 3)
76. Previous correct interpretations of the Supreme Court may need to be included in the Constitution.
77. If interpretation of the Constitution by the Supreme Court is to be legal, that fact should be included in the Constitution and not be usurpation by the Supreme Court. (e.g., Marbury v. Madison)
78. Select federal judges, including the Supreme Court judges, by lot after nomination by State Supreme Courts, not by Presidential appointment.
79. Relieve the workload of courts by using senior citizen members chosen in the same manner as regular jury members.  (e.g., for misdemeanors, family law, etc.)
80. Elected judges may not take campaign contributions from lawyers.  (Conflict of interest)
81. Election advertising for judges must be publicly funded.
82. Judicial appointments need an approval or disapproval time limit, such as one month.
83. More special courts are needed for technology, patents, etc.
84. Article III language should include; "serve during good behavior and health."
85. Move the Antitrust Department to the Judiciary.

## A. CONSTITUTION:

86. A common time limit clause is needed for amendment ratification.
87. Modernize vocabulary and capitalization.
88. Citizens' rights should apply to all States.
89. A convention should be a referendum choice.
90. The Federal Reserve Act or an updated summarized version thereof should be in the Constitution.  (e.g., the country does need a central bank)

91. Campaign finance rules (limits) need attention in the document.
92. The "commerce clause" is over used.
93. The phrase "promote the general welfare" needs explanation.
94. A more specific constitution will decrease lawsuits.
95. Define "high crimes and misdemeanors."
96. Should party rules be in the Constitution?
97. The "pay-go" rule should be in the Constitution.


## B. LAW (STATUTORY):

98. Grants, subsidies, and earmarks, if allowed, must be discussed and supported on the floor of Congress.
99. Limit the number of government employees as a percentage of population.
100. The "public use clause" of eminent domain laws is being violated. Doubling the payment might help.
101. The Education Department should be eliminated.
102. If pork remains, make the cost per State somewhat proportional to population.
103. All Federal laws should be carefully designated to avoid confusion with State law.
104. Anti-trust laws are not being enforced.
105. When regulators exceed ten percent of those regulated, the system is broke.
106. The funds designated for long-term social programs may not be used for other programs. (e.g., Social Security trust fund)
107. The Davis-Bacon Act of 1931 makes construction projects about 20 % more expensive.
108. Redistribution of income/wealth is stealing and violates natural law and religious teachings.
109. Appropriation bills need to be passed by mid-year, not October, and without numerous extensions. If not done on time the previous year's budget should automatically apply.
110. Ambulance chasing lawsuits should be restricted. Asbestos trial outcomes are inconsistent.
111. Except for active forestry, no individual or business may own more land than the area of the smallest State.
112. FDIC limits should be indexed to the GDP.
113. When three public polls rate the Congress below 20 %, a referendum needs to be called to vote for or against a new election.
114. New laws need an impact statement similar to environment laws so they are less likely to be challenged in court.
115. No pension monies (government or corporate) held in trust may be used for other purposes. They must be held in cash, high quality bonds, preferred stock, or mutual funds. (i.e., no derivatives, junk bonds, etc.)

116. Only one House should be allowed to introduce specific topic bills in order to eliminate duplication of effort. (e.g., technical, banking, insurance, etc.)
117. Honesty, ethics and morality are keys to fewer laws and regulations.
118. Overseas grants should never exceed U.S. grants.
119. State legislatures should nominate federal Senators as a compromise between the original Constitution and the 17th Amendment.
120. A low usury rate could be pined to the prime rate.
121. Limit the number of executive appointees and limit the time frame for their approval.
122. Many people want a flag burning law.
123. Security clearances need to go back only ten years.
124. Anti-trust must be consistent. (e.g., airlines versus oil giants)
125. Bank deregulation is risky, as has recently been affirmed (2008).
126. Stop-and-start government contracts cost extra millions of dollars.
127. The number of pages per year in the Federal Register is an indication of our excessive government.
128. Gerrymandering by States must stop. Use standardized near square or rectangular-like boundaries.
129. Medicare regulations and records are excessive. (110,000 pages, and that's before Obama Care)
130. No felon or DUI recipients in past five years may run for office.
131. The government should make no laws that do not apply equally to government workers, law enforcement officials, or even the President.
132. Grants to States should not require the receiving State to raise its taxes.
133. Consistency of drug legalization and enforcement is essential.
134. Pornography (naked or semi-naked humans in sexual or near sexual acts of arousal in any form) is forbidden and is not speech.
135. Agencies, commissions, and regulators making pseudo law must have final approval of the Congress.


## C. ADMINISTRATION (EXECUTIVE):
136. Why can't the Joint Chief take off his uniform and double as the Secretary of Defense?
137. Should the Justice Department be placed under the Judiciary or be a separate section of government as in some other countries? (i.e., to keep the administration honest)
138. What bureaucracy limits can be established?
139. Index salaries to the real GDP.
140. Use salary reduction to enforce accountability.
141. Upper level civil servants must rotate being supervision jobs to reduce ingrained control and corruption.

142. Executive appointments need a limit in number.
143. Government accounting practices must be as restrictive as those for corporations.
144. Improve (loosen) civil service firing rules.
145. Index and limit the number of civil servants to real GDP or population.
146. Should the Attorney General be an elective office as in some States? Or should he/she be nominated by the Supreme Court and approved by the whole Congress and serve during good behavior and health?
147. Limit the executive departments to a maximum number of ten, and return more responsibility to the States. (e.g., delete education, housing, etc.)
148. No Foreign Service chief officers should be political appointees.
149. The delay in approval of regulations is excessive which prohibits small company entrance into some fields. (e.g., drugs, vehicles, etc.)
150. Why is FEMA in the insurance business?
151. Government officials, employees, and officers are expected to set an ethical and moral example for other citizens.
152. No government department or agency, except the armed forces, should exceed in number of personnel over one-half the population of the smallest State.
153. All government office hours should be standardized as eight to five local time with the exception of field operations of military, intelligence and law enforcement.
154. For security reasons, bank processing should have at least two alternate, central type, organizations in the middle of the country.

## D. ECONOMY:

155. Coins should have more intrinsic value. (e.g., part silver)
156. No government bailouts without popular referendum.
157. Capitalism is our business mode and the preferred economic system.
158. Supplemental budgets must be discussed on the floor.
159. There should be an indexed limit on government spending.
160. Accounting rules (34 codes) rival the IRS in number and need limits.
161. The Federal Reserve needs to be audited periodically.
162. Fiscal policy is too "long-term" to stop recessions.
163. Transparent accounting is needed world wide for public trust.
164. The government must use fair tariffs to balance imports and exports.
165. Mixing of financial institutions should be prohibited. (e.g., for banks, insurance companies, savings and loan corporations, etc.)
166. Publish the preliminary budget summary on the Internet by the 1st of June and finish it by 30 July. October is too late and too close to elections.
167. Sinking funds (forward funding) must be established for future emergencies.
168. Hedges, derivatives, and swaps should be prohibited or closely controlled and if allowed must have excellent liquidity.

169. The government may not force mergers.
170. Minimum wage laws discourage entrepreneurship and reduce employment.
171. No more bank holding corporations.

## E. TAXES:

172. Code simplification is essential. The present system is way to voluminous and complicated. Limit the word count if nothing better.
173. No double taxation. (i.e., no corporate or death tax)
174. Withholding tax should be forbidden and paid by the individual personally.
175. No lawyer may vote for an Internal Revenue tax law unless they agree to give up the "bar" forever. It's a conflict of interest.
176. The tax code may not be used to generate political contributions.
177. Set a tax-free limit for churches.
178. Forced insurance, such as a Social Security tax, is not liberty.
179. Federal taxes should not exceed State taxes.
180. There needs to be a minimum tax so that all citizens are involved.
181. A national sales tax, except for food and medicine, should be considered.
182. Tax limits should be consistent and equal; e.g., ten percent local, state, and federal for a maximum of 30 percent, emergencies excluded.
183. A flat tax simplifies the system and decreases Congressional power.
184. No tax should exceed the cost of production for it leads to a black-market. (e.g., tobacco)
185. Higher taxes create avoidance.

## F. CORPORATIONS:

186. There should be a size limit. (see Chap. 5)
187. Set high indexed salary limits.
188. All corporate accounting books need to be public information.
189. To solve leadership problems, use the draft to replace civil servants with corporate leaders on a temporary basis.
190. Business leaders are not allowed to pick national candidates.
191. CEOs and the five highest executives of a corporation may not take compensation options or stocks in the near term. (i.e., it leads to a short run downturn in corporate stock prices)
192. Management pay may not exceed 100 times the company's lowest salary.
193. There should be better attempts to set international corporate rules.
194. Pro big efficient business does not mean pro huge or giant businesses or behemoth holding corporations.
195. Corporate size limits will cause large businesses to divest or split-up on-their-own prior to reaching a size limit, indirectly solving the near monopoly or oligopoly problem, as well as TBTF.
196. Both political parties have problems avoiding corruption associated with mega corporation lobbyists.
197. Corporate size and salaries could be indexed to the GDP.

198. The fewer the number of corporations in one industry the easier it is for them to collude and fix prices. (i.e., oligopolies should be discouraged with strict antitrust laws)
199. U.S. corporations should not invest in designated totalitarian countries.
200. There should never be just one company building a critical weapons system. (e.g., General Dynamics and aircraft carriers)
201. Anti-trust laws are not being enforced, a serious lobbying problem.
202. A single corporation should not have more employees than one-tenth the population of the smallest State. (i.e., it might get too-big-to-fail)
203. Depending on type, the efficient corporate size generally lies between the curves of best asset utilization and labor use maximization.
204. Corporations cannot renege on pension funds and must have cash or near-cash investments to cover at least 90 percent of future requirements.
205. Corporate welfare comes from the "general welfare" and "commerce clause' of the Constitution.
206. A size limit indirectly limits corruption.
207. Corporations frequently change their bylaws or charter, not every 200 years.
208. Citizens don't like too much power in too few hands.
209. Corporate spin-offs need to be studied as an indication of exceeding size efficiency. (e.g., what were the reasons for a spin-off?)
210. Only eight HMOs control the nations health system?
211. Conservatives want smaller government but not smaller corporations?
212. Politicians approve of larger corporations for campaign finance reasons.
213. Giant corporations become bureaucratic just like giant government.
214. Corporate size needs a better definition than just assets.
215. If capitalists aren't honest and moral---socialism will prevail.
216. The larger the corporations the more lobbyists. The more lobbyists the more corruption.
217. Vertical integration must be limited to one step up and one step down.
218. There should be a limit to what banks may owe each other.

## G. CAMPAIGN FINANCE:

219. Candidates must publish their résumé at least 60 days prior to the election.
220. No out-of-State money may be used for elections other than for the President and Vice President.
221. Campaign contributions should be limited and indexed to the GDP.
222. What campaign limits will be placed on opinion editors?
223. Without campaign finance limits, corporations will continue to be shaken down by candidates and other organizations.
224. House candidate contributions should come from the district represented and Senate contributions from the State represented.

## H. EDUCATION:

225. K-12 education must include civics, basic economics, the "social contract," and religious history.
226. Universities must teach western civilization, civics and different political positions on controversial social subjects.
227. No more take-home exams.
228. Abolish the Education Department. (It adds an administrative layer, fails audits, etc.)
229. Education of the justice system is essential.
230. Remedial classes in college are indirect double taxation for the public. (i.e., the subject was probably already taught once in high school)
231. Only 50 to 65 percent of each federal education dollar gets back to local school systems. (see 228 above)
232. Should full school taxes apply to people without children?
233. Teacher evaluations by students dilute grading accuracy and discipline.
234. As a second language, there should be an international standardized common language, such as Esperanto, to help solve the language problem worldwide and reduce teaching costs in many countries.
235. U.S. citizens need to be taught in high school to save for their own retirement and routine medical requirements.

## I. UNIONS:

236. No card check. Open shop is essential for liberty.
237. Unions want to take away secret ballots used in their organizations.
238. Government employees of all types (federal, state, local) may either join unions or vote, their choice, but not both. Voting to improve their conditions is a conflict of interest.
239. The federal government giving unions more power may cause States to rebel.
240. A specific union membership may not cross more than one adjacent State line.
241. Unions are prohibited from lobbying or contributing to more than their own State House or Senate members.
242. Judicial districts could be used to limit union size.
243. Restrictions on unions should be part of campaign finance reform.
244. All transportation modes are exempt from union strikes or slowdowns.

## J. MEDIA:

245. Anti-trust laws should be more restrictive for media companies than other corporations to reduce any possibility of purposeful propaganda.
246. Media radio, television, and print are too consolidated/concentrated.
247. The media must print, transmit, or show each candidate's résumé at least twice 30 days before each election.
248. Morality and mores requires strict pornography regulations by the FCC.
249. Freedom of speech does not include pornography or money.

250. The FCC should not be under direct executive or Congressional control.
251. The four or five radio conglomerates are too oligopolistic.
252. The media does not have sufficient overseas reporters to keep the populous properly informed.
253. Opinion writers should occasionally publish a brief self-résumé.
254. Out-of-State corporations may not control the five largest newspapers in any State.
255. The media should print and broadcast all ethical and moral transgressions of elected officials and appointed executive officers.

## K. VOTING:

256. We should be able to vote "none of the above."
257. "Winner takes all" is not in the Constitution.
258. In the computer age, fractional voting based on experience, education, etc., should be possible. (e.g., entrepreneurs, college graduates get 1½ votes)
259. A national referendum would be closer to true democracy.
260. The more taxes you pay, the more votes, or partial votes, you should get.
261. Voters on welfare have/are a conflict of interest.
262. Weighting votes would give more power to the middle and upper classes.
263. When registering to vote, the voter should sign a statement that he or she understands "the social contract."
264. Election day should be a half-day holiday.

## L. MILITARY:

265. A "purple" officer corps should apply to officers with the rank of Colonel (Navy Captain) and above and would decrease inter-service competition.
266. Military procurement needs better control and less Congress meddling.
267. Each State should have a minimum of two active duty military bases, two National Guard or Reserve bases, and one fully manned hospital in case of national emergency. (e.g., to spread the forces in case of a WMD attack and to distribute the federal money more equally among the States)
268. Since defense is the primary requirement of the federal government there should be a minimum amount of the real GDP in the national budget spent on the military, say four percent.
269. All of the military and State Department personnel need language training before going to a foreign country where we are trying to encourage or establish law and order and a democratic/republic form of government.
270. National service should be required of all able-bodied citizens. (see items 189 & 275)
271. A standing military force is motivated and appreciated more if all citizens participate.
272. The Joint Chief of Staff should be the Secretary of Defense.

## M. MISCELLANEOUS:

273. The Federal government is eroding States rights.

274. Should our States be rearranged; large ones split in two, such as California, or Texas, and small-populated ones combined, such as the Dakotas? Or should several States be combined into regions?

275. National service needs to be required. (e.g., a minimum of one year for all able bodied citizens taken in either the armed forces, peace corps, or other public service agency sometime before age 50; see 271)

276. Lobbying reform is essential.

277. A national ID card would reduce crime and improve administration.

278. Diplomatic immunity needs strict limits.

279. Witness tables in committee hearings should be at equal height to those of congresspersons. (i.e., no talking down to citizens)

280. No lobbyists offices physically allowed in Washington DC. (e.g., like no adult drinking bars near schools)

281. Are political parties obsolete? Do they have too much power?

282. Excess government land should not be given away to State or local governments, or corporations, or individuals, but sold at auction.

283. The existence of WMD and 9/11 means more government offices/departments should be moved out of Washington DC.

284. Government employees should be required to take an anti-racism oath.

285. Don't give foreign aid to countries that do not support the U.S. in the U.N.

286. Maximum retirement pay should not exceed one-half the pay prior to retirement.

287. Retired employees may not be rehired to their pre-retirement job and collect pay for both conditions.

288. Government correspondence may not use the phrase "government money" but must use "tax-payers money."

289. Reciprocal trade tariffs should not exceed five percent in either direction with possible exceptions for critical materials.

290. Should there be a maximum amount of land a citizen (like Ted Turner) or a business can own? (e.g., no larger than the smallest State, excluding forestry corporations)

291. If the U.S. is going to be the world policeman we should have more States in other parts of the globe.

292. Art is not speech.

293. Speeches in the U.N. should be in a universal language. (see item 234)

294. A universal language needs a section on universal religion using the common aspects of the present world religions.

295. Excessive regulations and taxes cause revolutions. (e.g., ours in 1776)

296. State legislators or State referendum should be able to recall their Federal legislators. All States should have such laws.

297. If all congressmen are millionaires, do we have democracy or aristocracy?

298. Taking from one citizen and giving to another is socialism and is a form of stealing forbidden by most religions.

299. It is possible to be a "progressive" conservative (more conservative) just as it is possible to be a progressive democrat or socialist.

300. Free or welfare housing doesn't work because the occupants have no incentive to maintain what they are given.

301. Welfare recipients must work at least part time.

302. Social programs should be left to the States as Amendment 10 suggests.

303. Both parties work together to protect incumbents.

304. Moving Congress to the Midwest would help keep lobbyists away.

305. If the federal government runs everything, why do we need State governments?

306 States are often coping out on social issues requiring the federal government to address sensitive problems.

307. Citizens have given the federal government an open-ended credit card with the 14th Amendment.

308. The U.N. is giving some of our money to China for forced abortions.

309. Smaller populated States should be allowed to combine some government functions.

310. If you can corrupt half of the small population States, you can control Congress. (i.e., small States all have two Senators)

311. People turn down employment to keep from losing their Social Security Disability (SSI).

312. State Governors should be more powerful than Federal Senators.

313. Is there already a fourth branch of government? (e.g., agencies that exercise some or many portions of the functions of the three main branches of government)

314. Legislators who flee their State to avoid a quorum vote automatically lose their seat.

# APPENDIX FIVE:  ECONOMIC ANALYSIS OF CORPORATE SIZE

This appendix is a supplement to support the Chapter 5 discussion of corporate size and efficiency.  It uses IRS data to show that giant corporations are not as efficient as we are often led to believe and actually may lead to higher retail prices than those of mid-sized businesses that are more competitive.

The IRS data breaks out corporation types or sectors and then places them in categories (1-12) according to average asset size with category 12 being the largest at $2.5 billion and over.  The following table gives calculations using the IRS data for return on assets (ROA), and salary efficiency ($\eta$), for eight corporate sectors plus an all-sectors column that also includes ten other sectors (not shown), such as agriculture and retail corporations.

The first row in Table 1 shows the number of category 12 (giant) corporations in the eight most interesting sectors.

Rows 2-5 show percentages for these largest corporations with respect to all the categories.  For example, for mining, the largest 45 (Cat. 12) corporations have 62 % of the assets of all mining corporations.

Rows 6 & 7 shows the category with the highest and best ROA (largest number) for the different corporate types (sectors).  Note that the highest ROA in mining is not the largest (Cat. 12) corporation but is for the smaller category 3 companies with only $500K to $1M in assets.  In contrast, rows 8 & 9, the lowest ROAs, include the giant finance and holding companies.

For salary efficiency ($\eta$) in rows 10 & 11 the lowest number (low is best) applies to category 4 (0.02) for holding corporations and categories 6, 7, & 8 (0.03) for construction companies.  The larger, less efficient salary numbers (rows 12 & 13), apply to category 3 of finance/insurance and real-estate/leasing.

The remaining rows apply to the combination of categories for the various sectors. Employee data comes from a different source as shown on the bottom of the table.

Table 2 of this appendix is a condensed set of mining data from the IRS data to provide a method of verifying the ROA and efficiency numbers in Table 1. For example for mining category 3: ROA equals income $904M divided by assets $2182M or 0.41 (using rounded numbers). For salary low efficiency in mining category 4 we have $1486 ÷ $12996 = 0.11. For all mining companies ROA is $58.8B ÷ $630B = 0.09. For additional raw data you must download it from the IRS referenced website.

The Table 3 GDP page provides an indication of economic trends. GDP is used as an indexing reference number in Chapter 4 and 5 for new constitutional language.

The Table 1 numbers appear to show that giant corporations, like big government, become more bureaucratic and less efficient. Although the analysis is very basic and ignores some of the complicating factors between and within corporations such as regulations and employee types, it does show that very large corporations are not all that efficient. The overall conclusion must be that limitations on corporate size are not unreasonable, but will reduce moral hazard and the dangers of TBTF, and that mid-sized or even large corporations may be more competitive than gargantuan and oligopolic companies.

## APPENDIX 5: TABLE 1: ANALSIS OF IRS TABLE 4, RETURNS OF ACTIVE CORPORATIONS, 2006*

| CORP → | TYPE (sectors) | All Sectors | Mining | Construction | Manufacturing | Transportation, Warehouse | Information | Finance & Insur | Real Estate Leasing | Holding (Management) |
|---|---|---|---|---|---|---|---|---|---|---|
| **Cat.12** | # Corps. | 2,568 | 45 | 16 | 343 | 21 | 107 | 1543 | 24 | 198 |
| % | Assets | 80 % | 62 % | 14 % | 79 % | 56 % | 86 % | 84 % | 19 % | 91 % |
| of | Salaries | 40 % | 44 % | 7 % | 73 % | 44 % | 62 % | 66 % | 19 % | 88 % |
| total | Income | 65 % | 61 % | 14 % | 54 % | 47 % | 101% | 72 % | 13 % | 83 % |
| | Taxes | 69 % | 64 % | 41 % | 70 % | 64 % | 86 % | 79 % | 19 % | 84 % |
| Highest | # | 0.21 | 0.41 | 0.24 | 0.09 | 0.17 | 0.04 | 0.41 | 0.12 | 0.i3 |
| ROA | Cat. | 2 | 3 | 2 | 2 | 2 | 2,8,12 | 2 | 2 | 3 |
| **Lowest** | # | 0.02 | 0.05 | 0.06 | 0.04 | 0.03 | (0.07) | 0.02 | 0.02 | 0.01 |
| **ROA** | Cat. | 12 | 9 | 9 | 7 | 10 | 4 | 8-12 | 3-8,12 | 8,9,12 |
| Best η | # | 0.09 | 0.05 | 0.03 | 0.05 | 0.10 | 0.11 | 0.07 | 0.09 | 0.02 |
| Salary | Cat. | 7,8 | 12 | 6,7,8 | 12 | 3 | 2 | 12 | 10 | 4 |
| **Low η** | # | 0.15 | 0.11 | 0.09 | 0.11 | 0.21 | 0.25 | 0.31 | 0.28 | 0.14 |
| **Salary** | Cat. | 2 | 4 | 2 | 2 | 10 | 3 | 3 | 3 | 3,11 |
| Over- | ROA | 0.03 | 0.09 | 0.09 | 0.05 | 0.04 | 0.03 | 0.02 | 0.03 | 0.01 |
| all | Salary η | 0.09 | 0.06 | 0.05 | 0.06 | 0.16 | 0.17 | 0.08 | 0.18 | 0.11 |
| Totals | Assets | 73.1T | 630B | 802B | 9.9 T | 630B | 3.2T | 34.7T | 803B | 15.5T |
| for | Income | 1.93T | 58.8B | 74B | 981B | 26.3B | 101B | 632B | 23.6B | 157.5B |
| Sector | Taxes | 353B | 10.7B | 8.3B | 101B | 7.8B | 26.7B | 68B | 5.6B | 41.8B |
| | Approx # Salary Employees | 61.4M @ $40K each | 385K @ 46.9K | 1.4M @ 57.4K | 9.45M @ 45.4K | 3.05M @ 40.5K | 3.1M @ 53.8K | 6.6M @ 46K | 1.5M @ 42.2K | 1.35M @ 90K |

Notes: The IRS Table 4 sectors are divided into 12 categories (cat.) with 12 being the biggest asset sector and generally with the highest income of that type of corporation.

The asset categories are:
Cat. 1, zero assets; Cat. 2, $1 to under (<) $500K; Cat. 3, $500K to < $1 M;
Cat. 4, $1M to < $5M; Cat. 5, $5M to < $10M; Cat. 6, $10M to < $25M;
Cat. 7, $25M to < $50M; Cat. 8, $50M to < $100M; Cat. 9, $100M to < $250M;
Cat. 10, $250M to < $500M; Cat 11, $500M to < 2.5B; Cat. 12, $2.5B and over.
Author's comment: additional categories would be useful.

Salary efficiency (η) is calculated by dividing salary dollars by total receipts or business receipts.
A lower number is better. For ROA (return on assets) a higher number is better.
Ten additional corporate sectors that are small, very competitive or already regulated are not included
Abbreviations: K = thousands, M = millions, B = billions, T = trillions

*Data Ref: www.irs.gov/pub/irs-soi/06co04ccr.xls (Jan 2010)
Approx. Employee data: www.bls.gov/oes/current/table2.pdf (Feb 2010)

# APPENDIX 5: TABLE 2: EXAMPLE RAW DATA (MINING)

| | All Cats | Cat 2 | Cat 3 | Cat 4 | Cat 5 | Cat 6 |
|---|---|---|---|---|---|---|
| Number of returns | 36,946 | 20,611 | 3,189 | 4,128 | 1,060 | 740 |
| Total Assets | 630,278,959 | 2,807,071 | 2,181,676 | 8,975,641 | 7,794,514 | 11,635,802 |
| Cash | 34621701 | 725,176 | 597,010 | 2,013,988 | 1,261,986 | 2,032,448 |
| Notes and accounts receivable | 83,088.121 | 345,767 | 276,657 | 1,424,842 | 1,131,070 | 2,116286 |
| Less: Allowance for bad debts | 493,632 | - | 16.700 | *7,593 | *3,823 | 22,565 |
| Inventories | 13,509,338 | *32,266 | *42,684 | 207,719 | 201,346 | 500,054 |
| U.S. govt. obligations, total | 1,223,592 | *16,556 | - | *4,933 | *63,379 | *19,192 |
| Tax-exempt securities | 733,933 | *8,147 | - | *166,813 | *214,504 | *184,057 |
| Other current assets | 18,.988,000 | 76,797 | 140,015 | 371,974 | 762,.980 | 631,651 |
| Loans to shareholders | 4,528,602 | 98,108 | 59,664 | 298,674 | 334,816 | 109,382 |
| Mortgage and real estate loans | 204,945 | * 25,334 | - | *97,447 | *21,369 | *2,181 |
| Other investments | 144,383,329 | 159,626 | 464,802 | 831,271 | 1,384,650 | 1,607,317 |
| Depreciable assets [25] | 211,501,113 | 3,445,759 | 1,310,895 | 7,400,402 | 3,964,432 | 6,095,848 |
| Less: Accum. depreciation [25] | 97.366,750 | 2,480,703 | 871,627 | 5,177,735 | 2,487,966 | 3,641,701 |
| Depletable assets | 219.352,850 | 761,689 | 243,746 | 1,562,954 | 908,291 | 1,885.341 |
| Less: Accumulated depletion | 67,947,809 | 539,171 | 173,611 | 908,227 | 475,262 | 780,806 |
| Land | 6.207,757 | 49,522 | 46,161 | 460,570 | 87,890 | 348,190 |
| Intangible assets (Amortizable] | 31,617,657 | 44,716 | 21,744 | 186,570 | 481,855 | 307,652 |
| Less' Accumulated amortization | 8,939,188 | 20,830 | 3,480 | 62,372 | 236,467 | 88,248 |
| Other assets | 38,107,400 | 58,313 | 43,717 | 83,690 | 182,464 | 329,526 |
| Total liabilities | 630,270,959 | 2,807,071 | 2,181,676 | 8,975,641 | 7,794,514 | 11,635,802 |
| Accounts payable | 55.456,266 | 109,905 | 237,750 | 863,326 | 851,332 | 1,531,389 |
| Mortg., notes, bonds less one year | 15,923,742 | 295,507 | 70,921 | 406,282 | 445,561 | 645,023 |
| Other current liabilities | 37,734,549 | 139,713 | 205,276 | 703,853 | 392,106 | 695,766 |
| Loans from shareholder | 6.712,489 | 672,841 | 235,819 | 818,631 | 621,020 | 542,158 |
| Mortg., notes, bonds, one year + | 139,014,810 | 1,110,109 | 402,582 | 1,270,053 | 986,362 | 1,452,240 |
| Other liabilities | 73.819,110 | 103,658 | 51,129 | 296,537 | 247,634 | 464,844 |
| Net worth | 301,618,194 | 375,337 | 978,199 | 4,616,960 | 4,238,500 | 6,104,582 |
| Total receipts | 366,513,788 | 7,314,234 | 4,672,125 | 13,983,708 | 8,046,806 | 12,430,157 |
| Business receipts | 327.272,187 | 6,997,985 | 4,404,292 | 12,996,109 | 8,120,566 | 11,529,761 |
| Interest | 4.999,401 | 8,507 | 7,551 | 34,426 | 29,043 | 40,651 |
| Interest on govt. obligations, total | 131,664 | *679 | *150 | 8,054 | 16,645 | 10,030 |

## APPENDIX 5, TABLE 2 CONTINUED

| | | | | | | |
|---|---|---|---|---|---|---|
| Rents | 555,874 | *7069 | *2016 | 27,807 | 6,748 | 11,319 |
| Royalties | 1,437,358 | *13,051 | *24,018 | 58,564 | 57,569 | 123,220 |
| Net S-T capital gain less net LT loss | 152,525 | - | *252 | *1951 | *751 | *1,707 |
| Net L-T capital gain less net ST loss | 5,214,139 | *31,092 | *59,423 | 166,044 | 103,751 | 129,181 |
| Net gain, non-capital assets | 4,257,376 | 53,673 | 68.337 | 170,880 | 131,582 | 156,051 |
| Other receipts | 18.666,494 | 201,705 | 104,748 | 506,158 | 378,857 | 422,814 |
| Total deductions | 308,901,236 | 8,321,000 | 3,767,530 | 11,609,807 | 7,508,923 | 10,891,690 |
| Cost of goods | 164,040,734 | 1,615,897 | 1,628,240 | 4,815,570 | 4,077,338 | 6,806,036 |
| Compensation of officers | 4,631,918 | 679,536 | 204.533 | 519,099 | 183.345 | 234,009 |
| Salaries and wages | 18.068,645 | 660,129 | 255,885 | 1,486,114 | 629,063 | 732,915 |
| Rent paid on business property | 6,140,839 | 323,330 | 154,790 | 547,041 | 216,720 | 224,860 |
| Taxes paid | 11.567,547 | 269.585 | 180,365 | 553,443 | 248,100 | 309,735 |
| Interest paid | 11.164,876 | 81,992 | 39,170 | 167,279 | 112,568 | 166,459 |
| Amortization | 3,244,849 | 5,947 | *1,108 | 36,299 | 18,415 | 36,585 |
| Deprecation | 15,288,357 | 288,122 | 148,804 | 517,997 | 365,446 | 508,109 |
| Advertising | 250,420 | 16,741 | 11,726 | 24,275 | 21,575 | 13,650 |
| Pension, profit-share, stock, annuity | 1,803,947 | 81,790 | 30,909 | 52,089 | 23,790 | 42,816 |
| Employee benefit programs | 3,720,841 | 74,942 | 28,835 | 199,999 | 78,239 | 96,165 |
| Net income (less deficit) | 58,844,799 | 992,555 | 904,445 | 2,365,847 | 1,321,238 | 1,528,429 |
| Income subject to tax | 44,645,947 | 104,643 | 138,321 | 377,696 | 317,731 | 464,068 |
| Total income tax before credits [7] | 15.598,316 | 26,534 | 41,921 | 123,299 | 108,466 | 159,620 |
| Income tax | 15,803,985 | 26,433 | 41,921 | 122,875 | 107,987 | 157,872 |
| Alterative minimum tax | 289,635 | *101 | - | *424 | *480 | 1,544 |
| Foreign tax credit | 4,171,916 | - | - | *97 | - | *9759 |
| General business credit | 123,729 | *395 | *35 | 117 | *304 | *827 |
| Prior year minimum tax credit | 555,330 | - | 3 | *91 | *118 | *2019 |
| Total income tax after credits [23] | 10,747,340 | 26,140 | 41,883 | 122,994 | 108,044 | 147,005 |

Endnotes at end of table section. Detail may not add to total because of rounding. See text for Explanation of Terms and "Description of the Sample and Limitations of the Data."

See bottom of Table 1 for reference. Numbers are in thousands.

# APPENDIX 5: TABLE 3: GROSS DOMESTIC PRODUCT

**Bureau of Economic Analysis**
**National Income and Product Accounts Table**
Gross Domestic Product
[Billions of dollars]
Last Revised on December 22, 2010

| Line | | 2005 | 2006 | 2007 | 2008 | 2009 |
|---|---|---|---|---|---|---|
| 1 | **Gross domestic product** | **12,638.4** | **13,398.9** | **14,061.8** | **14,369.1** | **14,119.0** |
| 2 | **Personal consumption expenditures** | **8,819.0** | **9,322.7** | **9,806.3** | **10,104.5** | **10,001.3** |
| 3 | Goods | 3,073.9 | 3,221.7 | 3,357.7 | 3,379.5 | 3,230.7 |
| 4 | Durable goods | 1,105.5 | 1,133.0 | 1,159.4 | 1,083.5 | 1,026.5 |
| 5 | Non-durable goods | 1,968.4 | 2,088.7 | 2,198.2 | 2,296.0 | 2,204.2 |
| 6 | Services | 5,745.1 | 6,100.9 | 6,448.6 | 6,725.0 | 6,770.6 |
| 7 | **Gross private domestic investment** | **2,172.2** | **2,327.2** | **2,295.2** | **2,096.7** | **1,589.2** |
| 8 | Fixed investment | 2,122.3 | 2,267.2 | 2,266.1 | 2,137.8 | 1,716.4 |
| 9 | Nonresidential | 1,347.3 | 1,505.3 | 1,637.5 | 1,665.3 | 1,364.4 |
| 10 | Structures | 351.8 | 433.7 | 524.9 | 582.4 | 451.6 |
| 11 | Equipment and software | 995.6 | 1,071.7 | 1,112.6 | 1,082.9 | 912.8 |
| 12 | Residential | 775.0 | 761.9 | 628.6 | 472.5 | 352.1 |
| 13 | Change in private inventories | 50.0 | 60.0 | 29.1 | -41.1 | -127.2 |
| 14 | **Net exports of goods and services** | **-722.7** | **-769.3** | **-714.0** | **-710.4** | **-386.4** |
| 15 | Exports | 1,305.1 | 1,471.0 | 1,661.7 | 1,843.4 | 1,578.4 |
| 16 | Goods | 906.1 | 1,024.4 | 1,162.0 | 1,295.1 | 1,063.1 |
| 17 | Services | 399.0 | 446.6 | 499.7 | 548.3 | 515.3 |
| 18 | Imports | 2,027.8 | 2,240.3 | 2,375.7 | 2,553.8 | 1,964.7 |
| 19 | Goods | 1,708.0 | 1,884.9 | 2,001.6 | 2,148.8 | 1,587.8 |
| 20 | Services | 319.8 | 355.4 | 374.0 | 405.0 | 376.9 |
| 21 | **Government consumption expenditures and gross investment** | **2,369.9** | **2,518.4** | **2,674.2** | **2,878.3** | **2,914.9** |
| 22 | Federal | 876.3 | 931.7 | 976.3 | 1,079.9 | 1,139.6 |
| 23 | National defense | 589.0 | 624.9 | 662.3 | 737.3 | 771.6 |
| 24 | Non-defense | 287.3 | 306.8 | 314.0 | 342.5 | 368.0 |
| 25 | State and local | 1,493.6 | 1,586.7 | 1,697.9 | 1,798.5 | 1,775.3 |

Source: U.S. Dept. of Commerce, Bureau of Economic Analysis
www.bea.gov/national/nipaweb.... Retrieved 28 Dec 2010

# APPENDIX SIX: ANTITRUST

The following is a partial list of some of the more important antitrust (competition) laws and Supreme Court cases.

Antitrust Laws:

1) 1890 Sherman Antitrust Act: This act is the first basic antitrust law. It prohibits restraint of trade, monopolies, or attempts to monopolize.

2) 1914 Federal Trade Commission Act: Bans unfair competition and deceptive practices.

3) 1914 Clayton Act: Adds to the Sherman Act. Prohibits mergers or acquisitions to substantially reduce competition or tending towards monopoly, interlocking directorates, tying arrangements, excepted unions, etc.

4) 1936 Robinson-Patman Act: Bans price discrimination or allowances between merchants.

5) 1945 McCarran-Ferguson Act: States regulate insurance except for specific circumstances addressed by federal law.

6) 1950 Celler-Kefauver Act: Closed Clayton loophole on asset acquisitions.

7) 1956 Bank Holding Co. Act: FDIC board must approve bank holding companies.

8) 1970 Newspaper Preservation Act: Exempted newspapers from some antitrust rules in order to save local newspapers.

9) 1976 Hart-Scott-Rodino Antitrust Improvements Act: Requires large contemplated mergers to notify the federal government in advance.

10) 1994 Riegle-Neal Interstate Banking and Branching Efficiency Act: Allows banks to branch across state lines if they support community needs.

11) 1999 Gramm-Leach-Bliley Act: Changed meaning of interstate branch bank and included out-of-state bank holding companies.

12) 2006 Deposit Insurance Reform Acts: Increased deposit coverage to $250K, established a range for reserve ratios, required studies, etc.

SELECTED EXAMPLE SUPREME COURT ANTITRUST CASES:[67]

1) 1899 Addyston Pipe and Steel v. U.S., 175 U.S. 211: Restricted federal antitrust to interstate commerce.

2) 1904 Northern Securities Co. v. United States, 193 U.S. 197: Antitrust Republican President Theodore Roosevelt use of Sherman Act to break up eastern railroads.

3) 1911 Standard Oil of New Jersey v. U.S., 221 U.S. 1: A major break-up of the tending monopoly in oil (approximately 90% control) that began in the 1870s. One dissent, by Judge Harlan, scolded the court for not being strict enough.

4) 1922 Federal Baseball Club v. National League, 259 U.S. 200: Exempted baseball from antitrust as not being an interstate business.

5) 1927 United States v. International Harvester Co., 274 U.S. 693: Effectively reduced the domination in harvesting machinery but the case dragged out several years and through the War and technology changes. The case reiterated that size alone or market power was not of itself illegal.

6) 1940 Apex Hosiery Co. v. Leader, 310 U.S. 469: Exempted unions from antitrust and refused to support local law or admit interstate commerce was involved. An inept conclusion.

7) 1943 Parker v. Brown, 317 U.S. 341: A California agricultural act regulating raisin sales (with interstate commerce involved) was ruled unanimously not to be within the purview of federal antitrust laws.

8) 1944 United States v. South-Eastern Underwriters Association: Allowed federal antitrust to apply to insurance; a reverse of previous findings.

9) 1948 United States v. Columbia Steel 334 U.S. 495: A five-four decision in favor of United States Steel corporation in acquiring another of many steel corporations. The dissent by Judge Douglas, quoting previous work of Judge Brandeis, was a logical tirade against the power of huge corporations.

10) 1966 United States v. Grinnell Corp. 384 U.S. 563: Grinnell and affiliates were broken-up and constrained. Two Judges dissented, questioning the economic expertise of the Court.

11) 1972 Hawaii v. Standard Oil of California, 405 U.S. 251: A State may not use federal antitrust law to protect its general economy.

---

[67] www.stolaf.edu/people/becker/antitrust…, St Olaf University lists 177 antitrust cases through 2004. The list is extensive but not all-inclusive. Retrieved 11 Apr., 2010

12) 1980/1987 Two similar State liquor cases (445 U.S. 97 & 479 U.S. 335): State price fixing laws are subject to the Sherman Act when States do not actively supervise their laws. Ruling was a change from Parker v. Brown above.

13) 1984 Copperweld Corp., et al. v. Independence Tube Corp., 467 U.S. 752: Five-to-three the Court changed a previous decision involving intra-enterprise conspiracy and ruled a wholly owned subsidiary to be part of a single company not able to conspire with itself. A non-competition agreement was ignored.

These cases should give the reader a rough idea of the Supreme Court's interpretation of antitrust laws since 1890. From St Olaf's list it can be noticed that the United States government as an instigator of antitrust cases has decreased significantly in the last few decades. This is a clear indication of the lax regulation since the Reagan era.

# APPENDIX SEVEN: JUDICIARY MINI PRIMER

To understand the Constitution it is important that the reader understand the justice system and particularly the Supreme Court portion of the Judiciary. The Constitution and the Supreme Court go hand in hand. The interpretation of our basic law (the Constitution) by that body, after all, "is law" itself, and adds to the foundation. The Supreme Court established their authority to decide which laws are Constitutional when Chief Justice John Marshall declared it to be so in *Marbury v. Madison* (1803).

The federal justice system of the United States is large and complex. The two basic elements consist of the Judiciary and the Department of Justice. Auxiliary parts of the Judiciary are buried both within the Justice Department and in the legislative branch.

The justice systems of the States are the backbone of total justice in the country, handling approximately 90% of all cases. Note, we are considering here only the federal system.

The Judiciary is a pseudo independent branch of the federal government and contains the main courts and judges of the federal system. It has approximately 35,000 employees and a budget of $6.7 billion (2010). The head of the Judiciary is the Chief Justice of the Supreme Court. Within the Judiciary, the Supreme Court proper has a budget of $88.5 million and 533 employees.

The Department of Justice is under the executive branch of the President and does law enforcement and litigation for the federal government. It is over three times larger than the Judiciary with 111,464 employees and a budget of 26.7 billion dollars (2010). The leader of DOJ is called the Attorney General.

The Judiciary branch courts are: 1) The Supreme Court; 2) The regional Appeals Courts; 3) The District Courts; 4) The Federal Circuit Court of Appeals; 5) The U.S. Court of International Trade; and 6) The Bankruptcy Courts.

Administrative offices of the Judiciary include: 1) The Federal Judicial Center; 2) Administrative Office of the U.S. Courts; 3) Defender Services; 4) Information Technology; 5) Security; 6) Sentencing Commission; 7) Buildings and Grounds; and 8) Trust/Retirement Fund Management.

The Tax Court, for some weird reason, is under the legislature and a so-called Article I court. The Marshals' Service handles the main security function of the Judiciary. United States Marshals have a long history with the Judiciary, going back to the original Judiciary Act of 1789, but were assigned to DOJ when it was established in 1870. A third much smaller organization with a direct relation to the Supreme Court is the Solicitor General. She/he works for the executive branch in the White House and often argues cases for the United States government in consultation with the Justice Department. For this reason the Solicitor General has a secondary office in the Supreme Court building.

Supreme Court Details:

1. The Judges: The nine Supreme Court judges are selected by the President and approved by the Senate. Most are Ivy League law school graduates and grew up in the Northeast. Almost all have had federal district or appeals court experience and many have clerking experience with an upper level court. They work hard reading cases and writing opinions dealing with hundreds of subjects for about ten months of the year and then take July and August off. The dynamics of the Court changes with each new member and several years may be required for a newly appointed justice to get fully comfortable with the job. They sign an oath card at investiture to support the Constitution and may keep their job indefinitely with good behavior (usually about 18 years). The Chief Justice is in charge of the whole Judiciary system and administrates it through the Federal Judicial Center. He also serves on several Washington D.C. boards, swears in new Presidents, and presides over the Senate in impeachment trials

2. The Clerks: The eight associate justices have four clerks (recent law school graduates) and the Chief Justice has five. The clerks read the eight to nine thousand petitions each year and write summary memos for the judges to assist them with selection of the 80 or so cases the Court will hear and decide. Clerks also do extensive research on petitions or "certs" (see glossary) for the justices and serve as a sounding board for discussion of cases. Leaks by the clerks to the press are not tolerated. These clerks are not to be confused with the Clerk of Courts. That is a separate office to handle administration.

3. Oral Arguments: Of the total one-hour oral argument, only 30 minutes each are allocated to the petitioner and the respondent attorneys. The justices ask questions nearly half of this time and they interrupt frequently leaving only about 15 minutes for each lawyer. The justices use the questions to indirectly communicate with each other. Only one other person is allowed at the table with each attorney. Podium lights control advocate speaking time. Oral arguments rarely change the decision of a justice ($\approx 5$ to 10% of the time), since they study each case prior to the hearing. The hearings are held in two-week sessions from October to April, beginning at 10:00 am sharp. No cameras or recording devices are allowed at hearings but the public is welcome as long as they remain quiet and respectful. Numerous camera requests have been denied.

4. Conference: Conferences without staff are used for final case selection (four votes required) and for voting on decisions. The decision conference occurs a few days after the oral hearing. After the decision vote the Chief assigns one justice to write the opinion if he is in the majority. If the Chief is not in the majority the senior justice in the majority makes the selection for writing the majority opinion. The justices take notes in conference to help with the writing of their position whether in concurrence or dissent. Justices exchange memos and as many as twenty drafts of an opinion are not unusual. Dissenters may join in a group dissent or write one on an individual basis. Historically, dissents have been useful in future cases.

5. Results: Unlike legislation, reasons must be given for the decision in each opinion. Five to four decisions occur only about one third of the time but do draw the most press attention. Unanimous decisions run in the order of twelve percent of the total. Cases do not always break on political lines since history and precedent are the primary considerations. Most decisions come out in December and January. When the Chief announces them, the public information office releases the written opinions. The time from oral argument to decision may be several months. Despite some bad decisions such as the *Dred Scott* case and the flip-flop examples in Appendix 2 and 3, the Court continues to hold the respect of the general public, even though the public has little knowledge of how it functions. Could the Court be better? YES!

6. Suggestions: The Judiciary is not truly independent as they claim because the Congress must pass their budget and the legislature has authority to establish additional courts as they choose. To provide true independence, the Court needs a budget based on a percentage of the average real GDP. Presidential selection and Senate approval is too political and needs revision. Independence from federal politics would be improved by using a rotating procedure and the State Courts for selection of federal justices, and State legislatures for approvals.

The number of cases accepted each year seems low as some of the justices admit. The Court should be required to accept a certain percentage of the petitions so they do not directly control their own workload.

Unanimous (9-0) decisions raise two questions. If they affirm the lower court, it indicates that perhaps petitions should not have been originally accepted. If they overturn, then the indication is that the preceding court did not do a very good job. At the other extreme (5-4) we have just one judge deciding for the whole nation what might be a monumental case. This does not seem reasonable and such cases should either be remanded for further research or confirmed by some other body such as a consensus of regional appellate court chiefs.

As for their present Judiciary budget—the portion with nearly one billion (2010) for appointed defense lawyers smells of excessive attorney pork. And five million for the Vaccine Injury trust fund is a strange item for a Judiciary budget.

With the complexity of modernization (see Appendix 1), no doubt the judges are overworked and perplexed with their science knowledge shortcomings. To solve this problem more specialty courts seems like a reasonable suggestion.

Finally, since the public is not well informed about the Courts, it is critical that all levels of education reinstate civics in their school curriculums. I hope this primer may be helpful in that regard.

# GLOSSARY --- JUDICIAL WORDS & ABBREVIATIONS

Judges and attorneys have a habit of using legal words with meanings that are often of Latin origin and other words that may have meanings not exactly the same as those in a common dictionary. If the reader plans on reading court orders or decisions and even the Constitution in places, this glossary may be useful. A good law dictionary can also be helpful. Abbreviations used in the book are at the end of the judicial words.

1. a priori: Common sense. Existing without experience.

2. ab initio: From the beginning. (Latin)

3. abrogation: Repeal of a law or custom in a lawful or formal action.

4. ad hominem: Argument linked to a person. (Latin)

5. adjudication: An act of a court making a judgment. Judicial decision.

6. amicus curiae: Friend of the court but not a party to the litigation. A petitioner may ask, or be asked, to submit a brief. (Latin)

7. appointments: The President appoints high level officials with consent of the Senate. (see Appendix 2).

8. assistance, writ of: A writ to enforce a court decree or to force a property title change, etc. One reason for the American Revolution.

9. attainder, bill of: An Act for punishment of a person or group without trial. The U.S. Constitution prohibits such Acts.

10. bill: A formal document. There are numerous types. A legislative law prior to enactment.

11. Black codes: Laws enacted after the Civil War (antebellum) to regulate newly freed slaves.

12. certiorari: A writ by an appellate court to deliver records for review. Shortened to "cert" by courts to indicate petitions submitted. To be better informed. (Latin)

13. corruption of blood: An obsolete and unconstitutional terminology. It prohibited relatives of criminals from inheritance.

14. cooling-off-period: An automatic delay in legal action.

15. capital cases: Serious offenses in which the death penalty is allowed.

16. clear and present danger: Likely exposure to certain and immediate harm. The First Amendment freedom of speech turns out not to be absolute. See Justice Holmes argument in *Schenck v. United States, 1919*.

17. comitatus: An able attendant. (See posse comitatus)

18. congruence and proportionality: The use of force must be consistent with the threat or grievance.

19. collective right theory: No such thing, rights are individual.

20. due process: Legal rules for protection of rights and prohibits the government from depriving a person of life, liberty or property. Refers to Amendments 5 & 14. (see Appendix 2)

21. dictum/dicta: A familiar rule, authoritative opinion, or judicial assertion.

22. devise: To plan or contrive. The act of using a will to dispose of property.

23. elastic clause: Another name for necessary-and-proper clause. (see Appendix 2)

24. eminent domain: The power of the government to take your property provided they pay you fair value. Abused on occasion. (see "takings clause" Appendix 2)

25. en banc: All judges present and participating (French)

26. enumerated powers: Listed powers of Congress specified in the Constitution.

27. equal protection: Every class of people must be treated the same. (Amend. 14)

28. equity (law/court): Natural or supplemental law and principles of justices dealing with common sense and fairness which do not depend on a specific statute.

29. escheat: Property reverts to the State when owner has no heirs.

30. estoppel: Generally stopped from doing something. Prevents an assertion previously concluded as legal. Lots of sub-meanings.

31. exclusionary rule: Any rule which excludes evidence. Illegal evidence cannot be used. Hearsay is suppressed. (See *Mapp v. Ohio*)

32. exculpate: Free from blame. An exculpatory contract to relieve liability.

33. ex parte: One side of an argument without notification of other parties.

34. expatriate: Withdrawal or removed from one's native country.

35. ex post facto: Done afterward. (Latin) An invalid retroactive law.

36. ex rel.: Relating to a suit brought by the government on application of a citizen.

37. fact vs. law: A real or actual condition versus its legal consequence or judication.

38. felony: A serious crime such as murder, rape, arson or breaking and entering. Usually punished by prison time or death.

39. founders: A group who start or fund a business or project. The Constitution was created by the Founding fathers, even those who didn't sign it.

40. framers: The drafters of a fundamental idea or concept.

41. general welfare: Provisions for well being through health, shelter, safety, etc. A very broad interpretation by the Supreme Court of Art. I, Sec. 8, Cl. 1.

42. habeas corpus: Requires a legal basis for holding a prisoner. You have the body. (Latin)

43. in law: There is a written rule of society covering the subject. A statute exists. In contrast to "in equity."

44. inclusio unius est exclusio alterius: The inclusion of one excludes all others. (Latin)

45. incorporation doctrine: The Supreme Court's habit of using "due process" to make the States obey parts of the Bill of Rights. Also called selective incorporation.

46. injunction: A court order to stop an action. Requires a good reason.

47. in forma pauperis: In the form or manner of a pauper (poor person).

48. in personam suit: Action to find out the obligations of parties. Against a person. (Latin)

49. in re: A judgment without parties. In the matter of. (Latin)

50. in rem suit: To determine rights with respect to property. Against a thing. (Latin)

51. irreparable injury: Money can't fix it.

52. intestate: A person who died without a will

53. Jim Crow law: Laws against blacks made unconstitutional by the 14th Amendment. (see Black codes)

54. just compensation principle: See eminent domain.

55. justiciable: A suit that may properly be brought before the court.

56. letters of marque: Written approval to attack others and take their assets. (e.g., to help stop pirates)

57. law: See "in law" above. A statute or constitution.

58. legislative veto: A legislative attempt to bar the executive from certain actions. (unconstitutional)

59. lex: Law. (Latin)

60. lex ferenda: What the law should be. (The purpose of this book)

61. lex lata: Current law. (Latin)

62. line item veto: An executive's power to void a portion of already passed legislation. (Unconstitutional as of 2010)

63. mandamus, writ of: When a superior court orders a lower court or government officials to perform their duties in the proper manner. (Latin, we command)

64. marque: See letters of marque, item 56 above.

65. misdemeanor: A less serious criminal offense such as larceny, shop lifting, etc.

66. money creation: The result from banks making loans or the purchase of government bonds outstanding. (The government generally does not just print money when the Federal Reserve feels like it.)

67. muckrakers: Teddy Roosevelt's early twenty century term for the press.

68. Miranda rights: The police must advise a suspected criminal in custody of their constitutional rights, e.g., the right to remain silent and have an attorney. (see *Miranda v. Arizona, 1966*)

69. natural law theory: Basic common sense rules of life, nature and morals without any government action.

70. necessary and proper: See associated clause in Appendix 2. Permits wide interpretation of the enumerated power of Congress.

71. necessities law: Objects required for living and including the enjoyment thereof. May include luxury items if you're a millionaire. (see Lever Act, 1919)

72. nulla poena sine lege: A valid law is necessary to punish. (Latin)

73. oath: An oral promise or statement of telling the truth. Possible punishment for violations. Several sub-meanings.

74. obiter dicta: A judicial holding from general observation. An incidental opinion.

75. oligopoly: Market concentration by a few large corporations and sometimes limiting competition.

76. one person one vote: Not what you might think. It has to do with population distribution and districts for government representation.

77. per curiam: By the whole court. (Latin)

78. per se rule: In antitrust law a violating practice that may do no harm. In and of itself. (Latin)

79. plenary: All qualified members in attendance. A full and complete complement.

80. pocket veto: If the Congress adjourns before the President's allocated ten days to sign a bill, and the President does not sign the bill, it does not become law. (Art. I, Sec.7, Cl. 2)

81. posse comitatus: A group of people called to help the sheriff or keep the peace. The so named Act prohibits using similar action with the U.S. Army without the President's approval. See comitatus above.

82. posterity: Future generations or progeny. That part of the Constitution preamble that the Congress ignores when they raise the federal debt.

83. post roads: Roads used to deliver the mail such as U.S. highways. In Constitution; Art. I, Sec. 8.

84. presentment: A formal legal statement. Congress presents bills to the President.

85. probable cause: Needed for evidence in a criminal case. Reasonable facts or suspicion. See 4$^{th}$ Amendment and *Beck v. Ohio*.

86. purse power: The House of Representatives controls the money (appropriations) in the Congress. (Art. I, Sec. 9, Cl. 7)

87. qua: In the character of, or as being. Just the way it is. In capacity of. (Latin)

88. quasi war: Similar to or resembling a real war. (Quasi is often used as a prefix)

89. reasonableness rule: A proper and fair condition under the circumstances. The situation is often difficult to determine and one good reason we have judges. Good facts in a tort, or obvious suspicion in a crime. See *Terry v. Ohio, 1968*.

90. redacted: Placed in the proper form without nasty words, etc.

91. red lining: Refusing loans or insurance to certain areas or districts. A form of credit discrimination.

92. rendition: States must deliver criminals back to the State with jurisdiction.

93. search and seizure: Usually associated with a judge's warrant and the constraining of a person under arrest or the securing of stolen property, etc.

94. separate but equal doctrine: Related to the way blacks were treated after the Civil War and supported by *Plessy v. Ferguson, 1896*. Later overturned by *Brown v. Board of Education, 1954*.

95. sinecure: Receiving pay with no work. Latin "without duties."

96. sine die: The item or meeting is adjourned with no continuation. Latin "without day."

97. sovereign immunity: The government is supreme and cannot to sued unless it agrees to be sued. Diplomats get special privileges and don't pay their traffic tickets!

98. stare decisis: Obligation to abide by precedents.

99. statute: A written law.

100. standing: The court will generally take your case since they have decided you have a right to make a legal claim.

101. substantial effect: Interpretation of law by judges. Used often to control the Commerce Clause.

102. tort: A non criminal wrong involving property injury and damages are sought.

103. to the contrary notwithstanding:  Lawyer double speak.  In spite of the conflicting condition or evidence this is O.K.

104. usury:  High interest rates on money or loans.  Early civilizations limited to about ten percent.

105. writ:  A written important document.  See writ of assistance or writ of mandamus above.

## ABBREVIATIONS:

1. AIG:  American International Group:  This is a huge insurance corporation deemed TBTF by the federal government during the 2008 recession.

2. AT&T:  A giant communications corporation broken up by the government.  A modern but less monopolistic version uses the same name today.

3. CEO:  Chief Executive Officer:  Normally the top person/manager in a corporation.

4. DOJ:  Department of Justice:  Part of the U.S. Executive Department and answers to the President.

5. FAA:  Federal Aviation Administration:  Controls civil aviation

6. FTC:  Federal Trade Commission:  Established in 1914 to prevent unfair competition and later given authority to make trade rules.

7. FDIC:  Federal Deposit Insurance Corporation:  From bank contributions insures the deposits of bank customers up to an amount set by law.  It also closes or sells bankrupt banks.

8. GDP:  The Gross Domestic Product is a measure of the production of goods and services by a country.  Real GDP is corrected for inflation to make comparisons from year to year.  The abbreviation GNP is now obsolete.

9. GSE:  Government Sponsored Enterprise:  A corporation backed by government law and money.

10. M-l:  Economic term/designation for money in cash or near cash.

11. M-2:  M-1 plus savings and time deposits, money market mutual funds, etc. (M-3 is now obsolete)

12. ROA:  Return on Assets:  A economic/financial ratio used to access a corporations efficiency and worth.

13. SEC: Securities Exchange Commission: Controls activities for efficient and fair stock markets.

14. TBTF: Too Big to Fail: A designation given to corporations whose failure would have a major disruption in society or money markets. The moral hazard of giant businesses.

15. UAA: Chapter 2 abbreviation for Unnecessary After Approval

16. UAE: Chapter 2 abbreviation for Unnecessary After Emancipation

17. UJNO: Chapter 2 abbreviation for Unnecessary, Just Needed Once.

18. UPOOE: Chapter 2 abbreviation for Unnecessary Part Of Original Establishment

19. WMD: Weapons of Mass Destruction. (atomic, chemical, biological)

# BIBLIOGRAPHY

MOST USED SOURCES:

Baldwin, Leland D., *Reframing the Constitution,* CLIO Press, 1972.

Bagehot, Walter, *The English Constitution (1867),* Cornell Univ. Press, 1971.

Hardin, Charles M., *Presidential Power & Accountability,* Univ. of Chicago Press, 1974.

Hazlitt, Henry, *A New Constitution Now,* Arlington House, 1942/1974.

Ketcham, Ralph (Ed), *The Anti-Federalist Papers,* Signet Classic, Penquin 1986.

Labunski, Richard, *James Madison*, Oxford Univ. Press, 2006.

Levinson, Sanford, *Our Undemocratic Constitution,* Oxford Univ. Press, 2006.

Mayhew, David R., *Divided We Govern,* Yale Univ. Press, 1991.

Meese, Edwin III, (Ed.), *The Heritage Guide to the Constitution,* The Heritage Foundation, Regnery Publishing Inc., 2005.

Miller, Jeremy M., "It's Time for a New U.S. Constitution." Southwestern University Law Review 17, (1987).

Napolitano, Andrew P., *Constitutional Chaos,* Nelson Current/Thomas Nelson Inc., 2004.

Ritholtz, Barry, *Bailout Nation,* John Wiley & Sons, Inc., 2009.

Robinson, Donald L., *Reforming American Government,* (The Bicentennial Papers of the Committee on the Constitutional System [CCS]), Westview Press, 1985.

Rossiter, Clinton (Ed.), *The Federalist Papers (1787),* New American Library, 1961.

Sabato, Larry J., *A More Perfect Constitution,* Walker & Co., 2007.

Stern, Gary H. and Feldman, Ron J., *Too Big To Fail,* Brookings Institution Press, 2004/2009.

Stid, Daniel D., *The President as Statesman, Woodrow Wilson and the Constitution,* Univ. of Kansas Press, 1998.

Sundquist, James L., *Constitutional Reform and Effective Government,* Revised Ed., The Brookings Institution, 1992.

Tugwell, Rexford Guy, *Model for a New Constitution,* James Freel & Assoc., 1970.
--------------------,*The Compromising of the Constitution,* Univ. of Notre Dame Press,  No
        date but approx. 1976.

Vile, John R., *Rewriting the United States Constitution,* Praeger Publishers, 1991.

Wilson, Woodrow, *Congressional Government,* Dover Publications, 1885/2006.
-----------------,*Constitutional Government in the United States,* Transaction Publishers,
        1908/2006.

SECONDARY SOURCES:

Ackerman, Bruce A., *We the People,* Harvard Univ. Press, 1991.

Aune, Bruce, *Kant's theory of Morals,* Princeton Univ. Press, 1979.

Aurelius, Marcus, *Meditations,* (Translated by Max Staniforth), Penquin Books, 1966.

Beck, Glenn with Kerry, Joseph, *Glenn Beck's Common Sense,* Mercury Radio/Threshold
        Editions, Simon & Schuster Division, paperback 2009.

Bennett, William J., *The Death of Outrage,* The Free Press, 1998.

Berkin, Carol, *A Brilliant Solution, Inventing the American Constitution,* Harcourt, 2002.

Blackstone, Sir William and Cooley, Thomas M., *Commentaries on the Laws of England,*
        Book the Second, 4th Edition by James D. Andrews, Callaghan &
        Company, 1899, (a reproduction).

Boortz, Neal and Linder, John, *The Fair Tax Book,* HarperCollins, 2005.

Bork, Robert H., *Coercing Virtue,* American Enterprise Institute, 2003.
-------------------, *The Tempting of America,* The Free Press, 1990.

Bowen, Catherine Drinker, *Miracle at Philadelphia,* Little, Brown and Co., 1966.

Browne, Harry, *Why Government Doesn't Work*, St. Martin's Press, 1995

Buchanan, Patrick J., *The Death of the West*, Thomas Dunne Books, St. Martin's Press,
        2002.

Chavez, Linda and Gray, Daniel, *Betrayal,* Crown Forum, 2004.

Chappell V. C., *The Philosophy of David Hume,* Random House, 1963.

Churchill, Winston S., *The Age of Revolution, Vol III, A History of the English-Speaking Peoples,* Bantam Books, 1963.

Coulter, Ann, *Slander,* Three Rivers Press, 2002.

Davis, Kenneth C., *Don't Know Much About History,* Perennial/Harper Collins, 2004.

Durant, John and Alice, *Pictorial History of American Presidents,* A.S. Barnes Co., 1955.

Elliott, William Y., *The Need for Constitutional Reform,* McGraw-Hill, 1935.

Ellis, Joseph J., *After The Revolution,* W. W. Norton & Company, Inc., 1979.
------------------, *Founding Brothers,* Vintage Books/Random House, Inc., 2000.

Ferguson, Niall, *The Cash Nexus,* Basic Books, 2001.

Garner, Bryan A. (Chief Ed.), *Black's Law Dictionary, 8th Ed.,* West Group, 2004.

Gingrich, Newt, *To Renew America,* Harper-Collins,1995.

Goldberg, Bernard, *Arrogance,* Warren Books, 2003.

Hannity, Sean, *Deliver Us From Evil,* Regan/Harper Collins, 2004.

Hart, Gary, *Restoration of the Republic,* Oxford Univ. Press, 2002.

Hayek, Friedrich A. *The Road to Serfdom,* Univ. of Chicago Press, 1944.

Henry, William R. and Haynes, W. Warren, *Managerial Economics,* Business Publications Inc./Dorsey Press,1978.

Hobbes, Thomas, *Leviathan,* (C.B. MacPherson, Ed.), Penquin Books, 1651/1985.

Hume, David, *Enquiry Concerning Human Understanding,* Henry Regnery Co. 1949.

Janssen, Sarah, Senior Ed., *The World Almanac,* Infobase Publishing, 2010.

Jefferson, Thomas, *The Jefferson Bible,* Beacon Press, 1989.

Kyvig, David E., *Explicit & Authentic Acts,* Univ. of Kansas Press, 1996.

Lamb, Brian et al., *The Supreme Court*, PublicAffairs, Perseus Books Group, 2010.

Lazare, Daniel, *The Frozen Republic,* Harcourt Brace & Co., 1996.

Lenin, V. I., *State of Revolution,* International Publishers, 1932.

Levin, Mark R., *Men In Black,* Regnery Publishing, Inc., 2005.

Limbaugh, Rush, *The Way Things Ought To Be,* Pocket Books, 1992.

Locke, John, *Second Treatise of Government,* BN Publishing, 2008.

Luttwak, Edward, *Turbo Capitalism,* HarperCollins Publishers, Inc., 1999.

MacDonald, Heather, *The Burden of Bad Ideas,* Ivan R. Dee Publisher, 2000.

Manning, Robert D., *Credit Card Nation,* Basic Books, 2000.

Mansfield, Harvey C., *Machiavelli's Virtue,* Univ. of Chicago Press, 1966.

McEachern, William A., *Economics,* South-Western College Publishing, 1997.

Medved, Michael, *The 5 Big Lies About American Business,* Crown Forum, 2009.

Mill, John Stuart, *Utilitarianism,* Henry Regnery Co., 1949.

Nietzsche, Friedrich, *Beyond Good and Evil,* (Trans. by R.J Hollingdale), Penquin, 1990.

Olson, Mancur, *The Logic of Collective Action,* Harvard Univ. Press, 1965/1971.

Montesquieu, Baron de, *The Spirit of Laws,* Prometheus Books, 2002.

More, Thomas, *Utopia,* (Trns. by Paul Turner), Penquin Books, 1965.

Perot, Ross, *United We Stand,* Hyprion, 1992.

Plato, *The Republic,* (E.V. Rieu, Ed.), Penguin Classics,1955.

Rachels, James, *The Elements of Moral Philosophy,* McGraw-Hill, 2003.

Rand, Ayn, *Atlas Shrugged,* Signet/New Am. Library/Penguin Group, 1957/1992.

Rehnquist, William H., *The Supreme Court,* W. Morrow and Co., 1987.

Rothwax, Harold J., *Guilty, The Collapse of Criminal Justice,* Random House, 1996.

Rousseau, Jean-Jacques, *The Social Contract,* (Trans. By Christopher Betts), Oxford Univ. Press, 1994.

Russell, Bertrand, *Principles of Social Reconstruction,* Routledge, 1916/1997.

Schlafly, Phyllis, *A Choice Not an Echo,* Pere Marquette Press, 1964.

Schlesinger, Arthur M. Jr., *The Almanac of American* History, Ed., Brompton Books Corp.,1993.
-----------------The *Vital Center,* Transaction Publishers, 1949/1998.

Schwartz, Bernard, *A History of the Supreme Court,* Oxford Univ. Press, 1993.

Singer, Peter, *Practical Ethics,* Cambridge Univ. Press, Second Ed., 1999.

Smith, Adam, *The Wealth of Nations,* Bantam Classic, 1776/2003.

Stein, Ben and DeMuth, Phil, *Can America Survive,* New Beginnings Press, 2004.

Story, Joseph, *Commentaries On the Constitution of the United States,* Abridged for School Use, Brown Shattuck and Co., 1833, (a reproduction).

Stumpf, Samuel E., *Socrates to Sartre,* McGraw-Hill, 1966.

Talley, George A., *The Constitution Triumphant,* Marcus Hook Press, 1920.

Thomas, Bill, *Club Fed,* Charles Scribner's Sons, 1994.

Tucker, Robert C. (Ed.), *The Marx-Engels Reader,* W.W. Norton & Co., 2nd Ed., 1978.

Wells, H. G., *The Outline of History,* (Revised by Raymond Postgate), Vol I, Garden City Books, 1920/1949.

Wilson, Andrew (Ed.), *World Scripture,* Paragon House Publishers, 1995.

Woods, Thomas E. Jr. & Gutzman, Kevin R.C., *Who Killed the Constitution,* Crown Forum, Random House, 2008.

# INDEX SUMMARY OF CHANGES IN THE CONSTITUTION

MODERIZATION (Chapter 4, Part 3):

- Newer Armed Forces names (e.g., Air Force) included (p. 79 & 84); Freeways and waterways added (p. 83); Forts renamed Bases (p. 84); Extended procurement times allowed (p. 84).

- Speedy trial defined (p. 79); The $20 jury trial updated (p. 80): Acceptance of legal tender (p. 83 & 85).

- The 30K population per representative revised (p. 81).

- Deletion of unnecessary establishment and obsolete civil war wording. (Ch 4)

- Removal of duplicate and repealed Amendment wordings. (Ch 4)

- Amendments folded into the main body of the Constitution. (Ch 4)


REVISIONS (Chapter 4, Part 3 & Chapter 5):

- Balanced Budget (p. 91)

- Ethics (oaths) Language Improved (p. 87 & 92)

- Campaign Finance Limits (p. 90)

- Debt (deficit) Limits (p. 91)

- House Terms Extended to Four Years (p. 80)

- Judicial Retirement Age Set (p. 88)

- Large Organizations Limited in Numbers of Employees and Assets (Ch 5, p.104)

- Term Limits (p. 80)

- War Powers Better Defined (p. 87)


Note: Ethics language and large organization limits are the author's suggestions. The other seven-revision bullets stem from citizen polls.

## MAIN INDEX (condensed)

## D D D

## E E E

## F F F

## G G G

## ABOUT THE AUTHOR

James Arthur Schmitendorf, born in 1933, grew up in Baldwin City and Lawrence Kansas. He graduated from the University of Kansas with a BS in Electrical Engineering and a commission in the USAF in 1956. After pilot training in single engine jet aircraft and a graduate degree in Electrical Engineering from the Air Force Institute of Technology he spent the remainder of twenty years in the Air Force flying aircraft in Alaska, Vietnam and the lower 48 for about ten years, and another ten years working as an engineer in missile intelligence and on the Minuteman Missile system. His master's degree thesis involved digitizing analog aircraft altitude information and combining it with a distance measuring transponder navigation signal. In Vietnam he was assigned to the Ninth Division of the Army of the Republic of Vietnam (ARVN) as the Air Liaison Officer and flew the 0-1 aircraft as a forward air controller.

Upon retirement from the Air Force as a Lt. Col., James (Jim) returned to college to obtain a BS in business from Black Hill State University in Spearfish SD followed by teaching fourteen years in the Electrical Engineering Department at the South Dakota School of Mines and Technology, retiring from that job in 1995. In second retirement Jim dabbles in old house restoration and motor vehicle technology as well as writing this book. He has three grown children and resides in Western South Dakota.

---

Please send constructive criticisms or suggestions to:
Jim Schmitendorf, PO Box 126, Piedmont, SD 57769